W9-BPK-041

You Can Quit

It's true. You *can* quit. As you read these very words, thousands of people have successfully quit crystal meth and are living drug-free lives.

That's just a fact.

If others can quit and be happy, then I can too. This was the great promise I held onto when I started my journey of quitting. I was a daily user who thought certainly I'd die with a pipe in my mouth or a needle in my arm. But if an addict as hopeless and lost as I was can quit, you can, too. And here's the best part. It doesn't mean your life will be hollow and sad, always jonesing for your one-time friend, crystal methamphetamine. No, your life can be better than it's ever been. As a survivor of crystal meth, you can live a life that's happy and free.

This kind of happiness is probably hard to imagine at the moment. I know that during those final months of using, I thought I'd never again experience the simple joys in life I once felt. Life had just become too dark, too empty. My very self—you might even say, my soul—had become hollowed out by crystal and its jealous demands. In the end, meth wants you all to itself. And it creates as much havoc and destruction as possible, sucking all the joy and pleasure out of life.

Quitting Crystal Meth is a book written by a recovering meth addict for meth addicts who are ready to begin quitting. It offers practical information and helpful suggestions for your journey of quitting. And quitting is a journey. But the destination is far beyond anything you can imagine now. Trust me on that. Trust the thousands of recovering meth addicts who didn't pick up again. There *is* a solution!

You'll hear the odds are against you. You'll hear outlandish statistics, that only a small percentage of us ever quit successfully. Cast that out of your mind. You *can* quit.

As you read these very words, thousands of people have successfully quit crystal meth and are living drug-free lives. You can, too.

Life is meant to be much more than what you're experiencing now.

Joseph Sharp

Timberland Regional Library
Service Center
415 Tumwater Blvd. SW
Tumwater, WA 98501
DEC 1 7 2015

Quitting Crystal Meth

What to Expect & What to Do

A Handbook for the First Year of Recovery from
Crystal Methamphetamine Addiction

Joseph Sharp

Acknowledgements

Thanks to the following people: Alan Downs, Ph.D.;
John Falcone; Bill LeGrave; Steve May; Marc-Pierre
Sanchis; Rev. Nancy Grissom Self; Nolan Willis; and
Bryan Wilmoth, BSW, CATC-III. I'm grateful for your
friendship and many suggestions to improve this book.

All rights reserved. No part of this book may be reproduced in
whole or in part without written permission from the copyright
holder, except by reviewers who may quote brief excerpts in
connection with a review in a newspaper, magazine, or electronic
publication; nor may any part of this book be reproduced, stored
in a retrieval system, or transmitted in any form or by any
means electronic, mechanical, photocopying, recording, or other,
without written permission from the copyright holder.

Copyright © 2013 Joseph Sharp

All rights reserved.

ISBN: 1477584633

ISBN-13: 9781477584637

LCCN: 2013901413

Createspace Independent Publishing Platform

North Charleston, South Carolina

Cover designed by Marc-Pierre Sanchis

For Theo,

and the addict who still suffers…

Contents

If You Are Buying This Book
for Someone Else...

If you are buying this book for a family member or close friend who has a problem with crystal meth, it's important to know a few things up front...

There is a physical, biochemical reason your friend or family member is addicted.

The medical community considers methamphetamine addiction to be a "chronic disease," just the same as high blood pressure or asthma. The difference between meth addiction and these other diseases is the location of the malfunction. With addiction, the malfunction is in the brain—so the illness affects feelings and behaviors. Because of this, those who don't know any better view addiction as a moral issue, a matter of willpower or character. But the truth is: addiction is a *biological process in a brain that is malfunctioning*. We don't blame someone with high blood pressure or asthma for the physical malfunction happening in their bodies. And we certainly don't shame them for seeking treatment.

Why is it different for the meth addict? It shouldn't be.

When you give this book to someone, remember there is no shame involved with addiction. It is a physical malfunction. It is not a sign that your friend or family member is somehow mentally weak or lacking in character. In my experience, the truth is often just the opposite. Addicts are some of the strongest people I know and can, when no longer immersed in their addiction, become people of amazing character.

When you give this book to someone, remember that only they can know when it's time to quit crystal meth. You can't make that decision for them.

The way to give this book is without any shame or blame whatsoever.

You give it because you care.

Chapter 1

Getting Ready

Here's a thought almost every crystal meth addict eventually comes to: "I want to quit, but I just can't. It beat me." When you realize you are powerless over the drug, you are finally being honest. This a good thing.

Here's the next thought many a crystal meth addict comes to: "I need help."

What separates those who quit successfully from those who can't is asking others for that help. Be it an addict who's traveled the road before you and is now in recovery, a treatment program, this book — or, perhaps, all three — you must learn to ask for help.

You don't have to die with a pipe in your mouth or a needle in your arm. You can quit. The journey starts here and now.

Whenever I look in the mirror, I burst into tears. What's happened to my life? It's a mess. I'm a mess.

— Brenda, 3 days clean

Quitting is like going to boot camp. It's awful at first, but then gets better. You have to jump off the cliff and just do it. One day at a time, do it.

— Joey, 9 months clean

A Question of Timing – It's as Individual as You Are

So you've decided to quit crystal meth. To begin with, you'll need to understand that there's no fixed recovery timeline that's universal. Depending on how long you used, how much, your sex, your age, and other health factors, you will experience quitting at a "pace" uniquely your own. When it comes to timing, and what you'll experience when, it's all variable.

As Associate Director of UCLA Integrated Substance Abuse Programs, Richard Rawson, Ph.D., developed a 5 stage model of recovery from cocaine addiction that is useful for our purposes here. Not only does this model accurately describe my own personal experience with recovery from crystal meth, it seems to generally fit the experience of most of the addicts I interviewed for this book. Adoption of the 5 stage model provides an easy way in which to accurately discuss the otherwise slippery process of recovery from crystal methamphetamine.

Each stage is connected to the physical and emotional changes that a person goes through as the body repairs itself from long-term substance abuse. So the first stage is, for example, pretty obvious—Withdrawal. What isn't so obvious is exactly how long this stage lasts.

The timeline used here is based on Dr. Rawson's original study. Therefore, for this book's purposes, the Withdrawal stage lasts from Day 0 through 15, about two weeks. But it's important to understand this is only a general estimate. Withdrawal can be as short as three days or as long as a month and, in some extreme cases, even longer. I'll remind you of these variations in each chapter, but it's good to know at the outset..

And to confuse matters more, sometimes you may experience the effects of two different stages simultaneously. This can often happen during transition periods between the stages. Also, how much time you spend in each stage will depend to some degree upon how active, both physically and emotionally, you become in your recovery. Many cofactors determine your particular timeline: your genetics, your activities, how long and how much you used, your sex and age, and other health factors, from depression to hepatitis.

Still, there are commonalities that most of us go through along the quitting journey. And there is some great advice on how-to quit from the many recovered meth addicts who've gone before. Again, when it comes to timing and what you'll experience when, this book can only give approximations. Remember, your journey of quitting meth is as individual as you are.

Do I Really Have to "Hit Bottom"?

The short answer is: no. Research shows that addicts who go into treatment only because they were forced to go – by the court or their families – have the same odds of getting and staying clean as the addict who has "hit bottom" and willingly seeks treatment on his own. The very same odds!

So let's expand the definition of hitting bottom for our purposes here. Traditionally, you "hit bottom" when external circumstances combine in such a way that something in your mind "clicks" and you think, "Enough of this!" As they say in AA, you suddenly become sick and tired of being sick and tired. But, in reality, people often hit bottoms without that subsequent "click of enough."

Let me tell you about my first bottom. I was hospitalized for a blood clot in my leg, due to my IV use of crystal meth. If the possibility of the clot traveling to my lungs or heart wouldn't make me hit bottom, what would? I was in the hospital for five days and firmly resolute that, after I left, I'd continue the clean and sober life with a program of abstinence and several Crystal Meth Anonymous meetings a week. I left the hospital hobbling on a cane, with an ankle and calf swollen to the size of a small watermelon.

I assumed this physical consequence would be enough to make me quit. Whenever I had the urge to use, I looked down at my monstrous "cankle" and remembered what a disaster my using had been. But it was barely ten days before the pipe was back in my mouth. The truth is, if hitting bottom was as simple as having disastrous consequences, health or otherwise, we'd all hit our bottoms and be done with it. My blood clot was, however, the beginning of the end of my using. It took three more months of stopping and starting, other mini-bottoms, but eventually sobriety stuck.

I know a woman who finally quit when she reached the very last moment of being able to keep her meth usage hidden from her family. She hadn't lost her apartment or job and was maintaining. Just barely, but still. And, true, her health issues were mounting. She knew the next run would push her over the edge to where everyone in her family would find out and all her friends would know. It was either give up hope altogether and fall into the deep dark void of meth, or stop now. She was at the precipice.

She told me if not for her aging parents, whom she knew expected her to take care of them one day, she would have just let the drug win, even to the point of losing her apartment and living on the street. But she couldn't put her mother and father through that suffering. Her older brother had died from meth use and she knew how much it would hurt her parents if they found out she too had this addiction. It would have broken them for the rest of their lives. This was enough for her to seek treatment and stop. But she went right to the edge, waited till the last possible minute to check into an outpatient rehab—which she chose over an in-patient so her parents wouldn't wonder why she'd disappeared from her life for 28 days. She was successful and is still clean today.

In AA they would call this a "high bottom," meaning she didn't have to sink so low as to be institutionalized or hospitalized. But it could just as easily be argued that it wasn't truly a bottom at all.

I know another recovering addict whose bottom only arrived when he found himself eating out of a Taco Bell trash bin for several nights in a row. Sitting on the floor of his apartment, which now had only a mattress and his laptop, staring at the used food cartons before him, he hit his bottom and felt "enough."

Whether you get to your own unique bottom (of a sort) or find yourself forced into treatment unwillingly, what's important is that, *at one point, you decide to actively participate in getting well.* Many a recovered addict began his or her journey to sobriety without hitting bottom, per se.

Get Family Involved – Quitting for Them Works, Too

Research proves that when your family or other loved ones are involved in your recovery, the chances for successfully quitting improve. In many cases, a person stops using because someone he or she loves wants them to quit. Take the example of Maria, a mother of two who used for over five years. After an intervention and a short time in rehab, it was love for her husband and children, and the obvious pain that her using caused them, that motivated her to stay clean during that tough first year. Getting sober for someone else—for your parents, your spouse or children, or any loved one—can be a powerful reason to stay clean, at first.

Family involvement can be a reminder that there is someone to get clean *for* and often makes for a more solid recovery. If appropriate and helpful, get your immediate and extended family involved in your recovery. Let one of the motivating factors to stay clean be the love you carry for them. In time, you will realize that you ultimately stay clean for yourself. But in the meantime, staying clean for someone you love can also help sustain recovery.

Detoxing Alone or With a Doctor?

It's best to do any detox under the care of a doctor, particularly one who is familiar with meth withdrawal. But since, for various reasons, detoxing under a physician's care isn't always an option, let's look at how you can prepare for your own at-home detox.

From a physical standpoint, crystal withdrawal is not dangerous—it won't kill you. You won't have seizures or delirium tremens, like you might from alcohol withdrawal. The main side-effects when detoxing from crystal, besides physical exhaustion, are emotional. Your mood will be low and you may have trouble experiencing pleasure. When this can become life-threatening is if that dark mood spirals into suicidal thoughts. If you are seriously suicidal, see your doctor or call 911.

I did my detox at home, as did about half the users I know. We basically slept for a couple of weeks, only getting up to wolf down some cereal, chug some Gatorade for hydration, or to use the bathroom. If your appetite is low, this is a good time to drink protein drinks or even that old tweaker standby, Ensure. Though, for most, the appetite quickly returns with a vengeance. This is a good thing.

Eat, eat, and eat again.

If you heavily use alcohol, marijuana, or any other depressants/downers, or opiates, it is recommended that you seek out medical supervision for your detox. Quitting *both* meth and depressants or opiates simultaneously can cause serious physical complications, like stroke, heart failure, and even death. If you are seeking a doctor to help you detox, I *strongly encourage* that you find a physician who specializes in "addiction medicine," as your General Practitioner might not be up on the latest advances.

Should I Consider Rehab?

Absolutely. Yes. If you have the opportunity to go to rehab, go! Here are a few good reasons:

1.) *Immediate removal from your using environment.* In the early days of quitting, it is good to be literally removed from your old using environment, including access to dealers, friends/acquaintances who use, and the external triggers in your life that can cause cravings.

2.) *Proper medical attention during detox.* Detoxing from crystal will be more comfortable in rehab because you'll receive medications to ease withdrawal.

3.) *Drug and mental health counseling.* You'll have mental health professionals and drug counselors working with you to assist in the larger process of living a clean and sober life. Also, you'll have group therapy with other addicts like yourself.

4.) *Training in new life skills needed to live a sober life.* Many of the pointers you'll read below will be covered in various presentations in rehab. You'll get a thorough understanding of what it takes to live a clean and sober life.

The biggest downside to rehab is that, as soon as you get out, you're right back in the environment where you once used, and you'll basically need to do all the things listed below as if you hadn't gone to rehab in the first place. Rehab is only the first stop along the journey of getting clean, but it's a great place to start.

Again, you're lucky if it's an option.

If you can do a full month—or, better yet, three—do it. Some insurance plans only allow for 3 to 5 days of in-patient detox, then switch to out-patient rehab. To my mind, this is less desirable than an extensive in-patient stay, but you still get the medical attention during detox and, afterwards, continued monitoring by specialists in addiction, even if on an out-patient basis. One benefit of out-patient rehab is that it forces you to face more immediately the issues of staying clean in the everyday "real world." But, all things considered, it's best to go to rehab for as long as you can.

Get a rehab out of town, if at all possible. Why? The more removed you are from your old using environment, the better. If you go to rehab out of town, you won't know any shady dealers or users. This new city means one thing to you, rehab, and so you are more likely to focus on your recovery. It's a lot easier to focus on your recovery when your dealer and party friends are hundreds of miles away.

(And if you want to improve the odds that you'll keep your sobriety through the first year, go directly from rehab into a "sober living" environment. There are sober living houses in most cities, representing a wide range of income—from shelters for homeless veterans to boardinghouses for Wall Street professionals.)

Now, if rehab is not an option, or just not right for you, know there are plenty of addicts who sobered up without it, including myself. If you decide to get clean on your own, you're still in good company.

Doing a "Geographic"

Doing a "geographic" is when you move geographically from one city to another, often a considerable distance away, in order to leave behind your using life. You wish to start with a clean slate, in a place where you don't know any dealers or have any using friends.

Because I now live in Palm Springs, a destination for many seeking recovery, I meet plenty of people who are doing a geographic. There's a lot to be said for this, though not many of us can afford to uproot ourselves from our families and jobs. As one former tweaker put it, "How could I afford not to? I'd already lost my job and alienated all my non-using friends. I knew that, after rehab, moving across the state and into a sober living house was the only chance I had to get my life back."

I know many successful recovery stories that begin by doing a geographic. I know just as many that end in relapse. Like rehab, a geographic move is only the beginning of your recovery. We "seasoned" drug addicts can get online or walk the streets and find meth in any new city, if we put our minds to it. The most valuable part of a geographic is the chance to begin again, to restart your life fresh and new. But as that old truism goes: *wherever you go, there you are.* You'll take your addicted self with you when you move. You still have a lot of work to do if you want to stay clean of meth. If you have the means to move to a city like Palm Springs or, really, any city with a strong recovery community already in place, it's something to consider.

There's a saying in AA that goes something like: All you have to change in life is one thing and that one thing is everything. Doing a geographic is a powerful way to start your recovery. Like rehab, if it's an option that is open to you, you're lucky. I'd say, go for it.

But it's not a necessity. The reality is, most of us get clean and sober without doing a geographic.

That Last Run

Often what we plan as our last run isn't, because we're not ready to quit yet. Here's my story. I decided that I had to quit and chose the date that I'd go into rehab. Two weeks before rehab I would begin my last run, which for me, usually lasted five days, followed by two days of sleeping. That would leave me a full week to detox myself, so I could be a star patient and show everyone how much self-control I had by entering rehab already clean. That was the plan.

(Feel free to laugh.)

So I did my run of five-plus-two days, then awoke to find, behold, I had another whole week before rehab. Of course, I didn't use those seven days to detox. What did I do? I partied right up until time for rehab (which I didn't end up going to, but that's another story). Still, this was my real last run, though not the one I'd originally planned. During that last run, I felt it. I knew in my gut and heart, this was going to be it—I'd have to quit or die a hopeless drug addict.

Why not start telling yourself that this run is indeed your "last," or, at least, near your last? You'll probably find it's not that easy to pull off. We are addicted, after all. One strategy: if you are planning to go to rehab, set an "intake" date at the rehab clinic and plan your last run right up until you check yourself in. If you are quitting without rehab, you can still follow the same plan. On the last day of your run, when you're exhausted, out of life and out of drugs, throw all your paraphernalia away (so it's really gone when you wake up), toss any crumbs in bags or bottoms of drawers, then crash and sleep. When you wake up, you'll be ready to do your own at-home detox/recovery.

Of course your best "last run" is the one that's already over. But we addicts don't tend to operate that rationally. The concept of a "last run" can get your mind prepared for the journey of recovery. It can allow you the time to do the other things in this chapter that will help you prepare to quit.

Trashing Paraphernalia

So you've just finished your last run. If you can clear your living space of any remaining drugs and all paraphernalia before you crash and sleep for a few days, you'll be ahead of the game. The trick, of course, is making sure these things get into a trash receptacle that will be empty by the time you wake up. If you've got all your pipes, syringes, and used baggies with crumbs stashed in your kitchen trash can, waiting for you to grab them in a moment of weakness, you'll do yourself little good. Go dump this crap in an outside trash bin that you can't easily access. Choose a bin that'll be emptied before you awaken. Choose a bin away from your home, at the back of a grocery store or large apartment house not your own. If there's no needle exchange program near, before trashing, put all syringes and points into an empty Gatorade bottle and seal the top. You don't want to accidentally stick someone who might be going through the trash bin looking for returnable bottles or food. Be thoughtful.

If at all possible, don't do this job alone. Have a sober friend or family member with you. It's easier to throw your old stuff away when you have support in doing it.

I suggest you *throw away everything* associated with your using. Toss the fancy torch-lighter you used, as well as the cool stash box. Dump empty baggies, straws, pipes, anything that you associate with using. Wipe out the drawers you kept your drugs in so there's no chance of coming across stray crystal chards or crumbs. Use Windex or some ammonia-based cleaner. Give that stash drawer a freshly-cleaned smell. Don't forget to clean out all those secondary stash spots, like backpacks, overnighter kits, or car glove boxes. Paraphernalia means *anything you used in your using rituals*. If you used a particular CD case on which to crush your crystal, or a certain small mirror, toss that, as well.

Here's the motto when it comes to deciding what is "using paraphernalia" and what isn't:

When in doubt, toss it out!

The less reminders you have of your using, the easier it will be to move forward with quitting. The sooner you can get your home clean of paraphernalia the better.

Of course, some of you will do this after you awake from your initial crash/sleep. That's okay. Better late, than never. Just make sure you do it as soon as possible, before the urges and cravings for the drug return in full force.

This will make your recovery a lot easier.

What About Marijuana/Alcohol Maintenance?

Almost every truly recovered addict I know had eventually to stop all mind-altering substances, including alcohol and marijuana—eventually. There's a lot to be said for going cold turkey and getting clean all at once. So let's encourage total abstinence from all recreational drugs up front. But, here comes the *But....*

In the real world, quite a few people prefer to choose the slipperier and potentially harder path of quitting meth *while* maintaining marijuana and/or alcohol use. In California, where marijuana can be legally prescribed by healthcare professionals, we call this "marijuana maintenance." I'll be honest, this is how I quit. While using meth, I smoked pot—mostly to help me sleep, and as a mood elevator when crashing. At the time, though total sobriety was the eventual goal, I believed I needed the emotional "cushion" marijuana offered me. Of course, after several months of being clean of meth, I realized I had a marijuana problem and had to quit that, too. At the beginning, it was easier for me to go on marijuana maintenance for a few months and then put down the pot.

Again, if you can, the best advice is to quit all drugs at once while under a doctor's care.

Also, here's the best reason *not* to choose the "maintenance" path: when you smoke pot or drink, your defenses are lowered and it's much easier to suddenly think using meth again would be okay. Many a meth relapse began with alcohol or pot weakening one's vigilance.

Is It Also Time to Quit Cigarettes?

If you smoke cigarettes now is also a great time to quit them. Not just because quitting is good for you—which it is—but because ditching cigarettes now actually increases your odds of successfully quitting meth.

Here's a tough statistic. If you smoke cigarettes, you have a 45% greater chance of relapse.

Why? Mostly because of chemicals added to the cigarettes that serve as "addiction boosters." These addiction boosters actually open up the same receptors in your brain that are affected by meth—meaning, you can get a bigger meth high if you smoke cigarettes while using. This means smoking cigarettes while trying to stop meth makes quitting more difficult. You're continually triggering those receptors in your brain into thinking meth is soon to follow. To put it simply, your brain associates the cigarette fix with a meth high.

In the long run, if you quit cigarettes at the same time you quit meth, you have a 25% better chance of staying off meth than those who keep smoking. So now is also the time to quit smoking cigarettes.

Finally, consider this. Since you are going to crash for a week or two anyway, you'll be sleeping during much of your early-stage cigarette withdrawal. That's really good news. I know people who quit meth and continued smoking cigarettes, but I know more who quit both together. Why not do your lungs and body a favor, and quit both at the same time? Besides, quitting tobacco will save you a lot of money, not to mention making your breath smell better.

Bottom line: though not absolutely essential, if you quit smoking cigarettes now, you will dramatically increase your odds at successfully quitting meth.

What About My Depression?

A surprisingly large number of meth addicts are also clinically depressed and were drawn to meth, in part, because it was a powerfully effective way to self medicate against their depression—at least, at first. It worked for awhile, before life became centered around crystal and before your tolerance for meth shot through the roof. If you have been diagnosed clinically depressed or suspect that you are, it's smart to get guidance from a doctor before you quit. There are several good drugs a doctor might prescribe that will help, to some degree, in keeping your depression in check as you quit.

As you'll read, depression and feeling like you're in a dark void of despair is a pretty common reaction to quitting crystal. But what you don't want to have is any additional depression on top of what you're already experiencing during those early months of recovery.

If you take anti-depression meds, don't stop. Speak honestly to your doctor about your plan to quit crystal meth. During this time, your serotonin and dopamine levels could use all the help they can get.

CMA and Other Programs – No One Is an Island

This book encourages you to get involved in the program of Crystal Meth Anonymous. If you live in a rural area where there are no CMA meetings, or if CMA is not right for you, you can just as easily attend the meetings of Narcotics Anonymous or, the mothership, Alcoholics Anonymous. I'll go into it in more detail—for example, on what to expect at your first meeting, how to participate or not—later. For now, I only ask that you keep an open mind to CMA and other programs.

Why?

Many reasons, but the best is this: it's at these meetings where you'll meet living, breathing examples of people who've quit successfully. At the Saturday morning "Happy, Joyous & Free" CMA meeting in Los Angeles, there are often more than fifty people in attendance with at least 2 years or more of sobriety. (Its usual size is well over one hundred recovering tweakers.) At the Thursday night CMA meeting in Palm Springs, it's not uncommon to find one or two people with over 20 years sobriety sitting in the room.

Yes, I know. Right now, 30 days seems like an eternity. But that's as it should be. I'm told it's often said at CMA meetings, "the first 30 days are the hardest." At meetings, you'll not only meet longtime survivors of meth, but more recently-recovering addicts like yourself. You can compare war stories *and* recovery stories. You will realize that your time of isolation and loneliness brought on by using can finally be at an end.

The simple truth is this: no one is an island. It's easier to quit if you have support for quitting. It's harder if you're alone. And harder still, damn near impossible, if you remain in the environment where others enable your using, instead of support your quitting.

A Few Words About Relapse

There's a lot more about relapse and recovery in this book's final chapter. But, for now, a few words are in order.

Not everyone quits on the first try. I didn't. It took me three months of seriously trying before I really, truly quit. I could give a lot of reasons, but the most honest statement about that time is: I just wasn't ready yet. I wasn't, as they say in AA, "sick and tired of being sick and tired." Despite walking on a cane with my leg swollen, I hadn't quite reached the bottom of my bottom.

But I was nearing it and knew this. So I kept trying to quit, over and over for several months, until I finally quit for real.

Relapsing is very common in the first month. That's the hardest 30 days you'll experience in your recovery. But, remember, thousands have done it before you, so you can too. The person who told you life was easy lied. Sometimes, it's difficult as hell. Sometimes, we go through relapse after relapse until we finally quit.

For others, they immediately put down the drug and the obsession is lifted—they never wish to pick up again. I hope that's true for you. But, if it's not...

Remember that relapse can be part of recovery. Especially at the beginning. Like they say in the rooms of all 12 Step programs: *just keep coming back*. Keep trying until you finally quit. It's only your life we're talking about, here. Nothing less.

Chapter 2

Withdrawal

0 – 15 Days

Withdrawal usually lasts from 1 to 2 weeks, but it can last upwards of 4 weeks—and, in some extreme cases, longer. Also known as the "sleep, eat, and drink" stage, your body and brain are in healing overdrive. There's a lot of damage meth caused that needs to be repaired before you can move forward.

For those first two weeks, all I could do was sleep and eat, sleep and eat, and sleep some more.

— Dana, 1 year clean

Just know you're not always going to feel this way. Have faith that it will get better, because it does.

— Steed, 7 years clean

WHAT TO EXPECT

The Crash – Into the Dark Void

One of the hardest parts of crystal meth withdrawal is what's called "the crash." Emotionally, it's that very dark mood coming at the end of a crystal binge—a depression characterized by sadness and hopelessness, on the one hand, and by rising anxiety or panic, on the other. Then add to this emotional hell its physical cousin, profound fatigue. Most likely, you haven't slept in many days. Most likely, you haven't been eating or hydrating properly, so it's no surprise your body craves rest and nutrition.

The crash is emotional and physical. And, other than prescribed medicines (or marijuana maintenance, which I do not suggest as a first choice), there is little you can do to alleviate the more severe symptoms other than sleeping and eating.

Just expect it. Know what's happening. Your brain's dopamine function is severely impaired right now. It may take a week or more to restore the dopamine to levels where your mood lightens, energy returns, and you have a clarity of thinking. Usually the crash lasts from three to fifteen days. But, for some longtime users, the crash may last upwards of a month or more. Remember, depending upon how long you used and how heavily, your body and brain have a lot of healing to do.

I know I was down for almost three weeks when I quit. By "down," I mean I felt like only sleeping, watching television, eating ravenously, and mostly wanting to be alone, in my bed. I forced myself to do some basic shopping for food, and pay bills, but little else. An addict from San Francisco whom I interviewed had a history of using meth for twenty years and reported his crash lasting over three months. Whereas a housewife from the Midwest, who'd used for just under a year, swore to me her "sleepy time" lasted three days, at most. Like most meth aftereffects, the duration of the crash depends upon a host of cofactors like how much and how long you used, your age, and general health.

Here are some other common meth withdrawal symptoms: teeth grinding, jaw clenching, and night sweats. And, in the meantime, your brain will be screaming for more meth.

To successfully quit, you must ride out the crash without picking up. That's what separates the men from the boys—or, the women from the girls. Try to remember that the crash will pass and is often followed by what's called the "Honeymoon" or "Pink Cloud." This is a very uplifting and joyous part of your recovery.

So, again, the goal of these first few weeks: ride out the crash without picking up. The silver lining—that Pink Cloud—is usually right around the corner.

Eating & Appetite

You are going to feel very hungry for the simple fact you haven't eaten much over the last few days. If you don't have an appetite at first, at least hydrate. Your appetite will return shortly—and with a vengeance.

Sleeping, and More Sleeping

You are going to need to sleep a lot. This is good. You can't sleep too much during the first couple of weeks. In the beginning, it's not uncommon for days to pass where you sleep around the clock, except to get up to use the bathroom, or hurriedly eat. If you're not peeing or eating, you'll probably be sleeping. Again, depending on how heavily and long you used, your sleep-fest will last from several days to, in some cases, over a month.

This is also where your meth-addicted brain tells you that the solution to all this physical exhaustion is to pick up and use again. The temptation is extreme, especially after a few days of solid sleeping. You erroneously think: Now that I've rested a few days, if I just had that little extra bump of chemical energy, everything could get back to normal. As one addict put it, "The life I always went back to was anything but normal. I couldn't sober up for more than a few days because I always used again so I wouldn't sleep my ass off."

The real solution here isn't more meth—it's more sleep. Remember, lots of sleep at this point of your recovery is a good thing. You can't get too much.

Confusion, Difficulty in Concentration, and Memory Loss

Depending on how heavily and long you used, you may have problems thinking and concentrating, and experience periods of confusion and memory loss. The most severe of these symptoms generally disappear as you complete detoxing. For now, just remember that *your brain is exhausted* both emotionally and biochemically.

Expect temporary confusion, difficulty in concentration and memory loss through the Withdrawal stage—and sometimes these extend, to a lesser degree, into the first few months of your recovery. Don't panic. It won't last forever. These symptoms are actually a sign that your brain is healing.

What About Hearing Voices, Feeling Paranoid, and Seeing "Tree People?"

If you regularly used high doses of crystal meth, you might develop "methamphetamine psychosis," which is a fancy way of saying your brain is temporarily sick from too much meth.

Here are some symptoms of this kind of brain sickness:

▶ seeing things or hearing voices (hallucinations);

▶ disorganized speech;

▶ feeling sensations such as bugs crawling on your skin or inside your body;

▶ elaborate paranoia—for example, the CIA, neighbors, or "tree people" are always just outside your windows, peering in.

Usually this kind of psychosis ends a few days after you've stopped using meth. But it can last weeks or, in some extreme cases, might be irreversible. And try not to panic, as these lifelong cases are very rare.

Here are some common hallucinations addicts experience: tree people, shadow people, beings lurking in your peripheral vision, voices that whisper from your attic or basement (even if you don't have an attic or basement), the sound of police helicopters approaching from the distance, aliens or ghosts speaking to you from within your television (whether it's on or not), the shuffle of invisible feet across your floor (or ceiling), the sound of that DEA or SWAT team just outside your door. You get the idea. Generally these auditory or visual hallucinations are dosed with a heavy serving of paranoia. Almost always, whatever thing you are seeing or hearing happens to be watching you too.

If you feel you are a danger to yourself or anyone else, see a doctor immediately. If you don't have a doctor, go to the emergency room. Why risk it? This way, the worst that can happen is you'll be put in the hospital on suicide-watch for a couple of days. Be sure to tell the doctor you are coming down off crystal meth, so he/she won't mistake you for run-of-the-mill paranoid schizophrenic. You are a meth addict coming off a run with too much crystal.

If you choose to ride out the hallucinations and paranoia at home, here's some information you should know:

▶ During methamphetamine psychosis your brain is hijacked and you are not in charge. The manic, paranoid tweaker in your head is running the show. And it is not to be trusted at all.

▶ The hallucinations and paranoia—the psychosis—usually ends within 2 to 3 days of quitting meth, but sometimes it can last upwards of a week or more.

▶ Finally, if your symptoms persist longer than ten days or get worse over time, call your doctor.

If you are in the midst of methamphetamine psychosis, most likely, you are not able to read these words.

If you are reading this for someone who is currently experiencing the above symptoms and has pretty much "broken from reality," you'll have to make the call for what to do. Bottom line: if you feel they may be physically dangerous to themselves or others, encourage them to go to the emergency room. And if you can't safely transport them to the hospital, call 911.

Emotional Surges – Tears, Angry Outbursts, or Both

Aside from exhaustion and a general sense of depression, you will most likely experience an emotional rollercoaster of sudden tears. Weeping at television commercials is common. A certain song plays on the radio and tears begin to fall. You are speaking to someone about something as ridiculous as the weather, but find yourself choking up with emotion. Just move through it. This is normal. It may last much of the first two weeks, or for several months.

Remember, your brain has been traumatized chemically. A lot has to happen to get your brain functions back into balance. Emotional intensity should become less over time, but it still may persist. All through my first six months, I could still tear up easily, especially when talking about my recovery or those I love.

Outbursts of anger are also very common in the first few weeks. Looking out from the darkness of the crash, it's easy to see problems everywhere and to become critical and judgmental.

One addict I interviewed during her first month of recovery told me, "If I'm not exhausted from it all, I'm so on edge I'll bite your head off. It's ridiculous and I know better, but just can't help myself. I'm constantly apologizing afterwards, which is even more exhausting."

Actually, this is the correct strategy—apologize and explain. I think it helps to prepare others for your sudden outbursts of anger. Let your friends and family know that you are angry and irritable with everything because you're going through Withdrawal. It's the side effects of the crash, not the real you, lashing out. Since your brain is not itself, apologize in advance and then try your best. Like much of this stage, it won't last too long.

Feeling Anti-Social

Most likely, the last thing you'll feel like is being social. The crash pulls you inward, into isolation. You certainly can't begin to share or empathize with others while in the first few days of recovery.

This is okay. Go easy on yourself.

Sleep, eat, and rest. Leave your important conversations until a couple of weeks have passed. Feeling anti-social during Withdrawal is perfectly normal and to be expected.

Abscesses, Staph Infections, and Meth Mouth

One addict who delayed seeing his doctor about an abscess on his arm, confessed, "Putting off the doctor was a huge mistake. Because I waited, I had to be hospitalized for two days on an IV drip." If you suspect any of your war wounds are becoming infected, or are refusing to heal within a few days, see your doctor immediately. It's foolish for you to try to handle these yourself.

The same goes for your teeth, if they are in bad shape. Don't wait. Make an appointment today—besides, it may take several days to get an appointment.

Proper treatment, dressing, and antibiotics can do wonders. We are in the 21st Century. Get some modern-day medical and dental treatment for those war wounds and you'll recover faster.

The First Month is the Hardest, Usually

It's said that one of the things you'll hear at almost any CMA meeting is: *The first 30 days are the hardest.* The best way to get through it is one day at a time. "That first month was definitely the most miserable," a lawyer from Beverly Hills told me. "I thought it'd never end. But it did." This is good advice.

"The first month is the hardest. Just get through it." If I've heard that once—or something close to it—I've heard it a hundred times. So expect this time in your recovery to be tough, but also remind yourself it'll only last a few weeks.

Here's an opposing voice to the "first month is the hardest" point of view. I've known more than one addict who said that, in less than a week, the crash lifted and they loved the first month. In fact, it was their favorite because they felt hopeful and clean of crystal for the first time in a long while. It's as if they went directly from a brief crash into a very Pink Cloud. If this is your experience, great. The less miserable your withdrawal symptoms can be, the better. Who am I to insist you have a hard first month? Just because most of us do!

Remember, the timeline of recovery is as individual as you are.

WHAT TO DO

"You just put yourself through hell.
Now it's time to love yourself."

— Maria, 5 years clean

Replenish My Body

The first thing you want to do is to break away from the "meth diet." This usu-ally consists of Ensure, Gatorade, and the occasional protein drink every other day. Here's what you need to do.

Eat: Start eating solid foods.

Hydrate: Drink enriched water, vitamin enhanced water, or, even better, coconut water.

Get your stomach back in shape: Try probiotic drinks like Kefir and yogurt. I especially recommend Yakult, a great product from Japan available in most major chain grocery stores.

Vitamins: Take a multi-vitamin daily. Maybe double up for a week. Also increase your potassium intake. Probably the best source is coconut water, but there are always bananas.

And, of course, the next best thing you can do for your body is to rest. Sleep, sleep, and more sleep. Let your body recover from the intense run you've just been on.

Calm My Mind

As with replenishing your body, resting is very important. This means not only sleep, but you also might want to rest your mind by "zoning out" with a marathon of your favorite TV shows or movies. "Thank God for streaming Netflix," one addict told me. "I spent my entire Withdrawal watching hours and hours of *Glee*."

Basically, you're just trying to get through the next week or two without stressing your body and mind any more than they already are. In this detox phase of your recovery, you may be depressed and, most likely, highly emotional. Your brain is desperately trying to heal right now. Try to give it a break and just zone out with something mindless from time to time.

And if you are quitting under the care of a doctor, she or he can tell if you need Ativan or Klonopin (and will prescribe a *limited* amount) to help calm you from the immediate physical and emotional distress of withdrawal.

Banish Shame

It's natural to feel ashamed of the mess your life has become because of this disease. But, if you are to survive, you're going to have to jettison any shame, at least for the time being. After you've moved through the initial stages of recovery, you will be able to address the damage you've done and find other ways to move forward responsibly.

For today, try to remember you have a disease. Your brain is still physically malfunctioning and *it's going to take time to heal*. It is crucial that you give yourself this time. Feeling shame can keep you in a loop—or shame spiral—where, instead of moving forward with healthy recovery, you become overwhelmed with guilt and keep relapsing. For the sake of your sobriety, you must banish shame from your life today.

Here's the blunt fact: shame is the great enemy of recovery, in both the short and long term.

Do Not Make Any Big Decisions

Now is not the time to make any of those "big" life decisions. In fact, you can't trust your decision-making process at this point because your brain is a mess.

Now is *not* the time to quit your job or end a relationship. Now is *not* the time to come clean to grandma about your addiction. Now is *not* the time to confess anything to anyone, period.

Just sleep, rest, and eat—for now.

Set a Sobriety Date

Figure out the date on which you were first clean and sober. I began counting mine at the beginning of my crash, after 24 hours had passed since I'd last used crystal. There are some cool phone apps for this. Search for "sobriety" at your app store.

Though some people don't like to count days, I think it's important—especially in early recovery. Just remember, in the first few weeks, every day is a big deal. Don't fret, it won't be this hard forever.

Counting your clean days is a good way to bolster your sobriety. The days will add up quicker than you think. And they're witness to the hard work you're doing to get and stay clean.

Chapter 3

The Honeymoon

Days 16 – 45 (up to 8 Weeks)

The crash has lifted, your body has made those immediately needed repairs, and you are feeling physically and emotionally much stronger. You might even feel great, better than you've felt in years. And it's only the beginning of the third week! Unfortunately, this upswing can lead to overconfidence and you might find yourself minimizing your past meth problem.

A lot of people will relapse here because of this overconfidence. But not you. You are prepared. You understand this Honeymoon won't last. Still, there's much to enjoy while it does.

And much to do in the meantime, while you're feeling stronger.

Finally, it gets a lot better.

— Ruth, 3 years clean

I have to remind myself: I have the only
disease in the world that tries to talk me
out of having it. It's constantly telling me,
"You're better now. You can control yourself
and party just one more time."

— John, 3 years clean

WHAT TO EXPECT

The Pink Cloud

"After about a week of feeling awful and sleeping all day, I woke up feeling great. It was like a light switch had been thrown in my brain and body. I had hope and energy back. I even found myself humming while taking a shower. I really felt the obsession to use had been lifted. I was suddenly so glad to be alive. I'd forgotten how great just an ordinary day can be." These words were said to me by an addict just one month into recovery and are an example of the "Pink Cloud," as the old-timers from AA say. It's a great time in your recovery and not everyone experiences it in such dramatic terms. Still, for most of us, this "Honeymoon" from our addiction happens to one degree or another.

Why? Again, the answer is biochemical and has to do with the brain. It usually takes a week or two to replenish the dopamine in your brain to acceptable levels. When that happens, your mood lightens and energy returns, along with some clarity of thinking. Liberated from your meth obsession, everything can seem suddenly happy, rosy, and wonderful. Hence the name, Pink Cloud.

Whether or not you experience this elation in all its glory depends on your individual brain chemistry. For some, there is no wide pendulum swing over to a big fluffy Pink Cloud. There's merely a feeling that life isn't as utterly hopeless as it seemed during the Crash. It's not as dramatic, but there's a definite upswing out of despair and exhaustion.

For most, the Pink Cloud lasts about a month. So, enjoy it. Now is a time to dive headlong into recovery. There are a lot of things to do at this stage in your recovery and we'll look at those in the next section "What to Do."

Use that newfound energy to go to CMA meetings, make new friends, and establish new routines and ways of living that support your sobriety. Put that Pink Cloud to good use and get fully active in your recovery. For now, however, there are some other things to expect during this Honeymoon period...

Dreams of Using Meth

You will probably begin to have "using dreams" during this time. I had about a dozen in the first four months. You may have many, or few. The first thing most people report from these dreams is that they awake feeling guilty—as if they actually used. That's normal. But after the momentary blip of guilt, try to feel immense gratitude for the reality that you didn't use. It was only a dream, thank God.

Dreams of using don't mean you're headed on the fast track to relapse. Dreams are your unconscious working out deeper issues.

If you want to dwell on these dreams, try looking at what else was going on besides your using. Who else was in the room with you? Did you hesitate before picking up? Or gleefully partake? Just note it—maybe write it down so you'll remember. Then, the next time you have a using dream, note how this changes. What is your dream telling you about how you *feel* about using, about what's happening *around* the use? This is far richer territory to explore.

Almost a year into my recovery, I dreamed I was offered a pipe and then I turned it down, got up and left the situation. When I awoke it was such a great dream to remember. My using dream was a not-using dream.

Most likely, you will eventually have not-using dreams yourself.

Memory Loss May Get Worse at First

During the early weeks after quitting meth, you may have trouble remembering things. Your memory may even seem to be getting worse. The good news is, depending on how long and how much you used, most of your memory will return after the first couple of months. Though some recovering addicts with long-term, heavy use report permanent memory issues, brain imaging has shown that this damage is usually reversible over time.

So, hang in there. Most likely your memory will start to get much better after a month or two.

What About Numbness from Injection Sites?

If you slammed your meth, you may have places on your arms or hands where you "missed" the vein and injected meth into body tissue by mistake. A small, hard knot often forms at these missed injection sites. The knot usually dissolves in a month or so, but you can quicken this process by applying heat—a heating pad or hot compress—so the capillaries will absorb the chemical residue into the bloodstream at a faster rate.

After the knot breaks, a patch of your skin and the tissue beneath it usually goes numb. How big the numb patch is and how long it will last depends upon how much meth was injected and, of course, the potency of the batch. Again, it's important to understand this numbness can last up to four months. Don't freak out if these patches of numbness take a while to dissipate, but they eventually go away. Try to have patience.

Triggers and Cravings

A song comes on the radio that you first heard while using. Or a person you once partied with walks out of the grocery store as you arrive. It can be as innocent as the straw a waitress sets next to your iced tea. Any of these people, places or things can trigger memories from your "old" life when you used. These memories—called *triggers*—usually lead to other *thoughts* about using. This thinking about using often evokes a longing that leads to a *craving*, an intense feeling in which you suddenly want or need the drug. If unchecked, *using* is often not far behind.

The sequence is: *Trigger... Thought... Craving... Use.*

Triggers are everywhere. You'll learn them, and then learn to avoid them when appropriate. For instance, the smell of bleach for one addict triggered memories of bathhouses and drug-fueled sex parties, so for the first year of his recovery he had to get rid of all the bleach in his apartment. For people who smoked cigarettes while high, smoking can be a troublesome trigger. The good news is that triggers often become less potent over time. The certain song that, in your first month, sent you into a mad craving tizzy may, after several more months, lose its power over you. With time, the potency of your triggers and the cravings usually mellow.

Successfully quitting meth has a lot to do with learning how to check these cravings and interrupt the sequence of Trigger-Thought-Craving-Use. (We'll look at some good strategies for this is the next section of this chapter, "What To Do.") For now, just know these triggers and cravings are to be expected. Don't worry—they can be dealt with successfully without relapsing. The fact is triggers and cravings are part of recovery.

WHAT TO DO

Remember: My Disease Wants Me Dead

A good way to think about your addiction is to personalize it. Think of your addiction as a living being, as "my disease," who has wants and desires. Whenever you get triggered, remind yourself that the "thought of using" is your "disease speaking" within your mind. And remember, "My disease wants to kill me." This motto or a variation of it—like, *My disease wants me dead*—can be a powerful affirmation whenever thoughts turn toward using.

In AA, people often say, "I'm fine while in the meeting. It's when I get to my car afterwards I'm in trouble. While I was sitting calmly inside, my disease was doing pushups out in the parking lot." I like this because it reminds me that, at any moment, even when the last thing on my mind is using, this disease can rear its ugly head. Try considering any using thoughts as the voice of your disease—a malevolent "other" who is out to harm you. This is closer to the truth than not.

Your disease has a lot of great lies to tell about how, now that you're a few weeks sober, you can use meth in a "controlled" way. Also, this disease is one of the few diseases in the world that tries to convince you that you don't have it. It says to your thoughts, again and again, "Your not a real addict. You can control your using, if you really want to."

It would be laugh out loud funny if it weren't so deadly.

It's crucial to realize your disease wants one thing, to kill you. During my first year, I said to myself at least once a day: "My disease wants only one thing, to kill me."

Keep the Goal of Quitting, Today

For some addicts, holding on to the idea that they are quitting "forever" is very important—we need that big goal. I am one such addict. To quit, I needed the grand promise that I was quitting forever, that my using days were definitely over and behind me. Crystal was to be banished from my life henceforth! If this works for you, great. Hold up that big prize and keep it in sight.

But not everyone thinks this way. And, even if you do, there will most likely be moments during your early recovery when you really crave a hit of meth.

At times like these, it might not help to think about quitting "forever." Here, it's better to think *in terms of days, sometimes even minutes or hours*. Come on, not using for a day is a lot easier than not using for a month!

Sometimes it pays to keep your goal of quitting small and easier to reach.

Don't set yourself up for failure if "quitting forever" seems too overwhelming. When I had a craving in my first few months, I would promise myself that, if I still had the craving tomorrow, I'd use then. Here was the bargain: I merely needed to postpone using today until tomorrow and *then* I could have one last party. (And I was serious—it was a real promise.) At first, this sounds like a recipe for relapse, right? Here's what happened. Every time without fail, when tomorrow came, I felt one thing—immense gratitude that I didn't use the day before.

Keep the goal of quitting small when you need to, but keep the goal of quitting for today.

Keep Other Small, Daily Goals

The goal of quitting is always first and foremost. Don't use. But you'll need other goals along the journey, daily goals you can accomplish and check off as you achieve them. Maybe one goal is to start going to the gym, and another to start some creative project like learning to paint or write, or bake.

Here are a few good small, daily goals for early recovery: *To stay awake all day* so that, at night, you begin to normalize sleep. *To walk briskly for 20 minutes out of doors. To sit in quiet meditation for 10 minutes*, a time you can lengthen as you get better at it. *To call three sober friends today* just to say hello, get out of your own head, and ask how their day is going.

It's important to make these goals small so that you can actually accomplish them. Remember, your primary goal is always: *to stay clean of crystal*. So, your other smaller goals should take a backseat. But, it's important to have them.

One of the primary reasons for relapse is boredom. You need to have goals that keep you busy. Keep other goals, but small goals.

Normalize Sleep and Routine

During withdrawal, the idea of needing medication to help you sleep is laughable. You're exhausted and have no trouble conking out. But as you move into the next month or so, you may begin to notice that, though you have no trouble napping in the middle of the afternoon, you do have trouble sleeping the entire night through. Anxiety and insomnia are often common nighttime experiences during these weeks. So it's important to normalize sleep as soon as you can.

You want to get off that "meth schedule" of staying up all night and catching a few hours, if any, during the day. You want to get back into the routine of the regular non-using world that sleeps at night and is awake during daylight hours. Normalizing your sleep allows you to focus on what's most important in day-to-day life.

Sleeping medication. Talk to your doctor if you want Trazodone, a nonaddictive powerfully sedating antidepressant, which is commonly prescribed for sleep. Personally, I like over-the-counter Benadryl. It tends to knock me out about an hour after I take it and I can sleep a good six hours. But there are all kinds of meds for sleeping and it's best to ask your doctor.

It is suggested that you do NOT take: Ambien, Sonata, and Lunesta which are "benzo-like" medications that target the same brain receptors as benzodiazepines. They are too easily abused and when taken in larger doses can cause psychotic symptoms, such as hallucinations. Been there, done that.

Again, ask your doctor's advice, but definitely tell him/her you don't want the "benzo-like" medications. Your doctor should know you are a recovering addict and prescribe appropriate medicines.

Recognize Triggers

Just about everything else you read in this chapter is going to be about how to avoid obvious triggers and/or counteract cravings. There are two kinds of triggers.

External triggers. These are things outside yourself that trigger a using thought. Like a text from an old using buddy. Or a certain online hookup site. Or the neighborhood where your dealer lived. We'll look at a few of the obvious ones and give you strategies to avoid them later in this chapter.

Internal triggers. These are triggers that originate from within you, usually emotions. Some people are triggered to use when very sad or depressed. You just want the low to be wiped away by the euphoria of the drug. Others, myself included, get triggered by just the opposite—joy and excitement. When something good happens, my disease tells me: "This is so great! Let's get high to celebrate and make this greatness last longer!" Some people are triggered when they feel misunderstood, criticized or ignored. Others when they get deeply angered, irritated, or feel embarrassed. Just about any strong emotion can be a trigger for you to use—if you associate using with it. Discover which emotional states trigger you the strongest.

Here is an important way to deal with any trigger…

Stop the Thought

Earlier in this chapter, we learned the sequence of *Trigger-Thought-Craving.* It goes like this: First, something *triggers* you to remember a time when you used. Next, you have *more thoughts* about using, perhaps glamorizing the party. This leads directly to the *craving*, that intense feeling where you want or feel the need to use now.

One successful strategy is to "stop the thought" dead in its tracks before you arrive at the craving. You interrupt the sequence before the thought of using can turn into a full-fledged craving. There are many ways to do this and I encourage you to find those that work best for you.

Here are some ideas:

Visualize the "thought" as a TV screen image, then change the channel. Picture the image of that using thought on a TV screen inside your mind. Then visualize yourself changing the channel of that inner TV. Pick a positive, happy image for the new channel—say, the image of someone you love dearly, hugging you. Or your favorite view of the ocean. Something powerful that instantly elicits happy feelings. So, you visualize this channel switch in your mind, and the new positive image appears on that inner TV screen.

Think of something that evokes a powerful emotion, like anger—but has no associations with using. One recovering addict told me he "stopped the thought" by immediately thinking of a certain politician who made him furious. Just rekindling his anger toward this politician (or political party) was enough to get his mind completely off using for the moment. Who knew politics could be put to such good use? (And, obviously, if anger is one of your triggers, you shouldn't try this.)

Snap that rubber band on your wrist. If the stop-the-thought process isn't working for you, try a preplanned action that interrupts the thought. Some rehab centers advise you to wear a rubber band around your wrist so that, whenever you catch yourself thinking about meth, you can snap the rubber band. This jogs your thinking process and stops the forward momentum toward craving and use. The sting of the rubber band on your wrist brings your thoughts back to the present moment.

But, say, you've moved past the thinking/glamorizing stage and are feeling a full-fledged craving. Here are some ways to counteract that craving once it's begun…

Counteract the Craving

The good news first: cravings will last only 30-90 seconds unless you start moving toward drug use. If you can wait it out, or counteract the craving, it will pass soon enough.

Say, you are triggered or have a pleasurable flashback, here are several ways to counteract the craving that follows:

Tell someone about it, now. Don't wait till later. Pick up the phone and call your "besty" or sponsor now. Get a phone list from a CMA or NA meeting and start calling until someone answers. They will be happy to be of service.

Play the memory forward to the bitter end. Don't just think about the euphoria of initially getting high. Jump ahead and play the memory forward to the bitter end. Remember how you felt *at the end* of your run. Remember those unsavory people with whom you were partying by the final days. Remember the desperation and loneliness. One recovering addict told me, whenever she had a using fantasy or craving, she immediately remembered that last week of using before she quit. Instead of having euphoric recall, she had "horrific recall." Remembering and re-feeling the horror of that last week of using was enough to bring her mind back into right thinking.

Go to a CMA or AA/NA Meeting ASAP. Don't wait till later. Go to the very next meeting. Just sit there quietly in the safety, or share. The main thing is to surround yourself with sobriety, as soon as possible. If there isn't a CMA meeting near, try NA. Also, in most cities, there is an AA meeting happening somewhere within the next two hours.

Surf the Urge. Cravings are a lot like wave swells in the ocean. They get bigger as they approach the shoreline, eventually reach a peak, then slide back into calm water. Another good technique to counteract a craving is to imagine yourself riding atop it like a surfer on a wave. You don't get down into the craving, but stay on the surface and ride the wave beneath you. Other thoughts will soon take over and, in 60 to 90 seconds, you'll be onto another thought. Imagine yourself surfing atop the urge until the wave dissipates and slides back into the calm.

Keep Your Feet Moving. If you can get through the moment, the desire to use will pass. Don't sit there stewing in the feeling/craving. Get up and get your feet moving. *Move physically and you will move emotionally.* Here's a short list of things you can do to take your mind off a craving: go to the gym, go to a coffee shop, force yourself to talk to a stranger, see a movie, play a highly-interactive video game, go dancing with a friend, take a brisk walk. The point is to get up, get moving, and distract your mind with a new behavior—those moving feet—instead of allowing that feeling/craving to turn into the old behavior of using.

These are just a few ways to counteract a craving. The main goal is always to truncate the craving—interrupt it with some learned, new behavior—before the desire to use becomes overwhelming.

Now, here are some proactive things to do in order to avoid triggers and minimize cravings beforehand...

Change Phone Number and Contact Info

The single best thing you can do for your recovery is to change your phone number. The next best thing you can do is change your email or, if you had a separate account for your using, delete it altogether. You don't want your old using buddies to be able to contact you. You want to leave them behind with that old life.

Delete All Using Contacts

You may think deleting old using contacts, including your dealer's, is something to be done before quitting. If you can do any of this beforehand, great. But, for many of us, we can't actually do these absolutely necessary actions until after we begin our recovery in full. That's why they are placed here, within the timeline of the first few weeks.

All those old using contacts need to be deleted. The dealers, the party buddies, the project tweakers. All erased so that you can't retrieve them. And don't forget to delete the phone numbers in your call history, as well.

Delete Social Media, Too

Sex hookup sites. Craigslist. Even Facebook. All social media that you employed in your using career need to be deleted. If your Facebook is overwhelmed with using buddies, create a wholly new account and send friend requests only to your non-using friends. Then delete your old accounts altogether.

Putting your hookup sites on "hold" or merely adding "HELL NO" to drugs or "NO PNP," is a slippery slope. It's best to delete your old profile, with all your old buddy lists, at once. If you keep your old username and all the partying buddies on your favorite list, what's the point?

If you are serious about your sobriety, you *must* delete your old party hookup accounts. *Don't do this alone.* Have a sober friend sit with you as you delete the accounts. Avoid the temptation to check the last emails and notices, just cancel your accounts altogether.

Only later, once you are many months into your recovery, or whenever you feel it's right, create a new account as a sober person. State in your profile that you are "in recovery" and "absolutely no partying or drugs." In short, give yourself some time away from the internet at the start of your quitting.

Nothing can take a person out quicker than an offer to party with a hot hookup. So don't let it get that far. Avoid all social media that intersected with your using and create new accounts that are for your sober life and friends.

When You Get a Call or Text from an Old Using Friend

If for some reason you can't change your number—and it needs to be a *very* good reason—here are some steps you can take:

Don't answer any unrecognized number. Once you delete all your using contacts from your phone and computer, don't answer any calls that come through with only a number identification—it's probably an old using buddy. Let all unknown callers go to voice mail. Screen your calls.

Respond by texting only. So a using friend calls and leaves a message. Don't call back and speak to them. Respond with a text. Something like: "I no longer party. It was affecting my health. I wish you well. Peace." Keep it short, sweet, and *do not invite a response.*

Delete incoming and outgoing phone and text histories. Don't forget to delete any record of that call/text from your using friend. Be vigilant about this. You don't want their number to be stored anywhere that you can find later. Remember to delete both incoming and outgoing histories. Thinking that you don't have to delete this history is actually setting the stage for relapse.

Change Old Patterns & Routines

Old hangouts of your using days should be avoided now that you are clean. Find a new coffee shop if you met your dealer at the old one. If you live in a state that allows over-the-counter syringe purchases, go to a different pharmacy, one where you've not purchased points. Do you regularly run into old using buddies at a local grocery or convenience store? Then it's time to change these routines. Do you pass a house you used to party in as you drive to work? Change your route to work, even if it means taking a longer way. You are trying to change any old patterns and routines that might trigger a craving.

Perhaps you always listened to a certain radio station when you were high. I went through a two month period where I couldn't listen to any dance mixes because it took my mind immediately back to using.

If you drank Gatorade and sports drinks while you partied, switch to brands you never used, or to more healthy alternatives like vitamin-enriched or coconut waters. Certainly avoid that particular 24-hour McDonalds you always tweaked at. Try another McDonalds. (Or maybe something better for your body like Subway.) You may find you have to change a lot of your routine. This is okay.

You are changing your life. It's no small order.

It won't always be like this. When I lived in Los Angeles, I used to drive near my dealer's house a couple of times a week. There was just no way around it. I'd obsess about it as I neared the intersection, then hold my breath as I passed. This went on for about four months into my sobriety. Then one Sunday morning, I ate lunch with friends at a restaurant right around the corner and didn't realize I was a block from my old dealer's apartment until walking back to my car. I'd spent and entire hour within a hundred yards of the room I'd bought and used in for months—and none of this crossed my mind. I just ate lunch and enjoyed the time with friends. So your triggers do change, do lessen over time. That's the good news.

Move (or Redecorate)

If you used heavily in your neighborhood, move as soon as you can. And don't move into another neighborhood where you also used. That defeats the purpose. Bottom line: if you can move from the place you used in to another apartment, another neighborhood, or even city, do it.

If you can't change your living situation, the next best thing is to redecorate. I'm serious. Especially change up your bedroom, if you often used there. Make your new non-using environment wholly different from that place where you used meth. A new coat of paint, a rearranging of furniture, new bedspread—all this works wonders. You are trying to lessen the triggers you encounter on a daily basis. Start with your living space.

Also, the same goes for any space where you once used. If you used in an office at work, rearrange that office. The goal is to create life anew.

Find a Besty With Whom I Can Be Completely Honest

When triggered, one of the best things you can do to counteract it is to "tell on yourself." That means talk about it with someone—give them the gory details of your flashback, craving or fantasy. You'll be amazed at how confessing to a craving will lessen its power over you. For your sobriety, it's crucial that you find a best friend with whom you can be completely honest.

If you are working a CMA program, this person will be your sponsor. But even though you tell your sponsor everything, I think it's good to have another sober friend with whom you can come clean. The more sober friends you have who understand, the better. When we keep our urges to use secret, we're far more likely to relapse.

One evening, out of nowhere, the thought crossed my mind that on my next trip into Los Angeles, I could have a one-night party. (After all, I'd been sober over six months at that point, didn't I deserve a little reward?) So within ten seconds, I planned what lie I would tell my friends in Palm Springs, the lies I'd tell to my L.A. friends who thought I was coming to visit, planned exactly where I'd stay to party, from whom I'd buy the drugs (online) and exactly how much I would pay for an eight ball. Really. In a matter of seconds. My monkey mind ran with it, planned the whole thing out.

In maybe ten more seconds, I was floored by guilt. Immediately, I extended the thought to include how awful the end of the party would be, how I'd feel when I crashed the day after—then I realized, who was I kidding? I'd never partied for just one night in my life. My usual run was 3 to 5 days, always 5 toward the end. No, if I used, I'd party 5 days then crash briefly and rationalize that, since I've lost my sobriety already, I might as well party for a while longer. And so the cycle begins. I might go on another year-long run, or worse. When my mind played thorough this possibility I was relieved because the urge to use, the sudden fantasy, had been busted. Still, I knew what I had to do.

The next morning, I took two sober friends aside and confessed the whole thing to take away any power that it might hold if I kept it secret. I eventually shared about it at a group level later in the week, disempowering the fantasy even more. Having a friend, or several, you can share everything with is crucial to sobriety. Because we have to learn not to shame ourselves when our disease rears its ugly head. It's not a weakness of character to be triggered or get lost in a using fantasy. It's what the malfunctioning brain of an addict does—craves more drugs.

How we treat that craving is the key. Don't keep it secret. Take away your disease's power over you by "telling on yourself."

Practice an Elevator Pitch for Saying "No"

In Hollywood, the "elevator pitch" is that short and sweet sales pitch (usually for a film) that is succinct, well-practiced and to the point. You always have your pitch at the ready, in case you happen to find yourself standing one day next to Steven Spielberg in an elevator.

For you, the elevator pitch is that immediate and practiced response you'll give to someone who offers you meth. This particularly applies to people from your using days who you might encounter on the street, at the grocery store, online, or even in an elevator.

Whenever asked if you want to party, give your elevator pitch immediately and without reservation. Here are some examples for you to tinker with and make your own:

"No, thanks. I no longer party. Crystal almost destroyed my life. So, again, no."

"No. I really have a problem with crystal and have decided to stop. As my friend, I know you'll understand. So please don't talk to me about it again."

"No, thanks. Crystal was really messing with my health, so I'm not partying any more."

Find your own elevator pitch and *memorize it*. Then you must PRACTICE YOUR PITCH, saying it forcefully and without reservation.

Practice, practice, practice. Imagine various scenarios where someone asks you to use with them, and practice saying your pitch. This is a great exercise to do with sober friends. Role play and take turns pretending to be that favorite dealer you've accidentally met on the Gatorade aisle at Albertsons. Take turns asking each other if you'd like to use, then practice your response. Get really good at your "no, thanks" pitch.

This way, if the situation occurs where someone offers you crystal, you'll instantly respond with a well-practiced elevator pitch that flows quickly off your tongue.

And then get the hell out of that elevator, fast.

Schedule a Dental Exam

Here's one of the single most important gifts you can give yourself in sobriety. As meth addicts, we usually have very bad dental hygiene. Do it now. Call and make that appointment.

Get Professional Help – Drug Counseling vs. Traditional Therapy

If you can work with a therapist or counselor who specializes in addiction, consider getting some professional help, as well. This is not the time for "traditional" psychotherapy, however. Now is *not* the time to dig into yesteryear's childhood traumas to understand how they affect your relationships today. Instead, now is the time to focus on relapse prevention skills, on how to cope with cravings, and avoid triggers and so on. While understanding your troubled childhood may be important in the longer run, it's not helpful now and may even be harmful.

In these early months of recovery, you don't need the additional stress involved in deep, exploratory therapy. Quitting crystal and learning how to keep clean is the task for today. And, believe me, that's enough. Save the deeper inquiries for later.

Ideally, you would want a drug counselor/therapist who is experienced in working with crystal meth users. But if you can't find one in your area, a general addiction counselor can still be helpful to your growth. The basic problems of addiction are universal regardless of the drug. Today you need someone in your corner who understands addictive behaviors and is trained to help you overcome them.

The difference between a counselor and a traditional therapist is: a counselor will tell you what to do; a therapist will listen to you. At this point in your recovery you need to be told what to do. (If you seek out a therapist now, as opposed to a drug counselor, I recommend you find a therapist who specializes in dialectical behavior therapy or cognitive behavior therapy with an emphasis in drug recovery.)

You had bad habits when you were using. You were accustomed to zero structure. But in your recovery, you'll need to form good habits. Counselors teach good habits and they teach you structure. And, most importantly, they teach you to believe that structure is a good and safe thing.

Attend a CMA Meeting

Last, but certainly not least, one great way to help you stay clean is to start going to CMA meetings. I've heard it said by more than one recovering addict that, in their first few weeks, it was only when at a meeting that they felt calm, only then did their mind stop racing. In the early weeks of recovery, you might find that meetings offer the same calming effect for you.

The next chapter explores the pros and cons of CMA meetings and tells you what you can expect if you go to one. So please keep an open mind. And now, everything you always wanted to know about CMA but were afraid to ask...

Chapter 4

CMA Meetings

What It's All About

The simple truth is this: It's easier to quit if you have support for quitting. It's harder if you're alone. And harder still, damn near impossible, if you remain in the environment where others enable your using, instead of supporting your quitting.

Get to a meeting. Take a desire chip. Get a
sponsor.

— Theo, 15 years clean

There's a saying we have in AA and CMA. It
goes, "Meeting-makers make it." I used to
turn my nose up at that one, but over this
last year, I've watched four people with
longtime sobriety go back out. And I mean
longtime sobriety, each having well over
five years. The one thing they all shared
in common? Each had stopped going to
meetings on a regular basis. Life was just
too successful and full that they no longer
found time to prioritize a meeting within
their weekly schedule.

— Deborah, 8 years clean

It is so okay to ask for help. I didn't think it
was at first and I was wrong. Ask for help.
How else are you going to get it?

— Carol, 7 years

WHY THESE MEETINGS?

The Pros

You might not be a "crowd person" or "joiner," but it doesn't matter. You certainly don't have to be either to get great benefit from a CMA meeting. Here are some pros:

You'll meet living, breathing people who have been successful in quitting. This lets you know that, in fact, quitting is possible. It's not just a theory, but reality. Also, if you have any questions about your recovery that this book doesn't cover, most likely you'll find an answer from someone who has gone through it before.

A meeting is a great place to make new non-using friends. Where else are you going to have a room full of people who are like you, addicts trying to quit? Most likely a using friend is one of your triggers. But the new friends you make at meetings should support you in trying to quit.

You'll be able to "speak out" those thoughts you bottle up about using and recovery. It's at meetings where you'll meet someone who's gone through what you're currently experiencing—say, you just had a using dream and are feeling guilty because you enjoyed it. You can commiserate or, at the least, have a sympathetic ear. Also, "telling on yourself"—for instance, telling aloud about that impulse you had yesterday to phone your dealer, or whatever—is a great way to take your power back from your disease. Your meth addiction wants you to keep many secrets. It's those secrets that will often take the newcomer out again.

If you have something you need to share, but don't want to do it on a group level, then pick someone who has some time under their belt and go up to them after the meeting and say, "I really need to talk. Would you be willing to listen?" Most likely, they will be honored.

The Cons

It's rare that it happens, but the biggest downside to a CMA meeting is the same danger you have whenever you get a group of newly sober tweakers together—the possibility that someone might ask you to use with them. I've never had anyone offer me meth at a meeting, but I know it's happened. And though you can be asked to use anytime anywhere, a group of newly sober addicts are particularly vulnerable. Again, it will probably never happen to you, but it's the dark little secret that needs to be talked about. The meeting should be a sacred space, but the reality is predators exist. I've even known of a dealer who once came to a meeting in search of new clients. So remember, though the room is filled with a lot of solid sobriety, it's also peppered with struggling addicts. Just a concern to keep in mind.

Other, lesser cons…

Some newcomers complain they feel "left out" because almost every person in the room already knows everyone. They greet with kisses or hugs, calling out to one another by name. Of course, the upside is that, if you stay around, soon you'll be one of the people who gets hugged and called by name too. Meetings challenge you to get out of yourself, take risks, and meet new people.

If you are terminally shy, it will be more difficult. But only more difficult, not impossible. And, once you introduce yourself, you'll never find a group of more accepting people.

Another common newcomer complaint is: "These meetings depress me because people whine and bellyache so much." There's always an excuse for what's wrong with a meeting. Too many people. Not enough people. Too many tweakers. No tweakers, just a lot of AA drunks and me. Too many people share. Not enough people share. And so on. It's at times like this when it helps to remind yourself: *I have the one of the few diseases in the world that tries to convince me that I don't have it.* The disease in your mind is working overtime telling you: "I don't belong here at this meeting, with these people."

Remember, your disease wants you to keep away from meetings at all costs. It wants you to avoid all the things that are good for your recovery. It desperately wants to convince you that you are now well and can party responsibly, just on weekends—you know, like you did once, a long time ago. It'll come up with a lot of excuses to keep you away from 12 Step meetings.

Other Fellowships – AA and NA

For various reasons, you might not be able to go to a CMA meeting. Perhaps there's not one in your area or, say, it meets only once a week. Or, perhaps, being in a room full of former tweakers is too triggering for you.

I've met a few addicts who couldn't go to CMA meetings because they always left the meeting with cravings. Something about the meeting triggered them profoundly. If this is you, then AA or NA (Narcotics Anonymous) will work better. Though, after enough time has passed and you're not so easily triggered, you might want to try CMA again. There's nothing like a room full of "your people" to make you realize you're not in this journey of recovery alone.

Isolation is the big enemy.

Every successfully recovered addict I know will tell you, almost immediately, they didn't do it alone—in fact, they couldn't have done it without the support of friends or "the fellowship" of CMA, NA, or AA.

A word about AA: Most AA meetings ask that you identify solely as an "alcoholic," period. They ask that you keep your "meth addict" identity to yourself. This is because, in the early days before CMA or NA, many AA meetings were overrun by addicts seeking help. I know many tweakers who go to AA meetings and in their mind substitute "meth addict" for alcoholic. You'll find the similarities between the meth addict and the alcoholic are many and the differences few.

Just attending the meeting is the important thing. You're in a room with people who understand, people quitting along with you. A meeting reminds you, you are not alone.

WHAT TO EXPECT AT A MEETING

"Hello, my name is X, and I'm a crystal meth addict."

These are the words that open every CMA meeting. The leader introduces himself or herself and then self-identifies as a crystal meth addict. At one point near the beginning of the meeting, introductions will go around the room and each person announces some version of "I'm [name] and I'm a crystal meth addict." Or "tweaker." Or sometimes just "addict," especially if the person has other drug programs they're working. It's also fine to simply say, "[your name], meth addict." When there's a large room, sometimes brevity is appreciated, though not required.

The only requirement for attending a CMA meeting is the desire to quit using crystal meth. Period.

If you can't go alone, you can always have a friend go with you. If your friend is not an addict, he or she can simply self-identify as: "I'm [name] and I'm here to support [your name]."

The Typical CMA Meeting

Most CMA meetings last one hour and follow a similar format. It always opens with the leader for the meeting—there's usually a different guest leader every week—announcing, "Hello, my name is X and I'm a crystal meth addict." That's when the group answers back, in unison, "Hello, X." Often the meeting continues with the Serenity Prayer.

Then the leader usually adds, "I have identified myself as a crystal meth addict. Are there any other crystal meth addicts present?"

This is when everyone in the room raises a hand. As a group, we all self-identify as crystal meth addicts. You don't have to say anything here, only raise your hand. (If you can't raise your hand, that's okay, too. But you are a meth addict, so why not?) There's tremendous power in self-identifying. You take power back from your disease, an illness that demanded secrecy from you for so long. You are no longer ashamed.

Often, this is when the leader announces: "If there are any newcomers who are in their first 30 days of sobriety, please raise your hand and state the nature of your disease. We do this not to embarrass you, but so we can get to know you better."

Now you can either raise your hand and self-identify with "I'm [your name] and I'm a meth addict" or not. Sometimes it's just too overwhelming to self-identify. Often when you first start going to meetings you just want to sit in the back and participate minimally. That's fine. There are no rules on "how to" attend. But I would encourage you to raise your hand and tell the room you are a newcomer. Because, the only way you are going to start making new non-using friends at meetings is to identify yourself—and newcomers get special attention, because we all remember how difficult it is to go through those first 30 days.

Next usually comes the "Selected Readings" portion of the meeting. Examples of these readings are "Am I a Tweaker?," "The 12 Steps and How They Work," and "What is the CMA Program?" These readings are usually printed on laminated sheets handed out to different people before the meeting begins. So it's possible you might be asked to read aloud one of these when you first attend. (It's considered an honor—no one is trying to put you on the spot.) Just know you can always say, "Thank you, but I'm new and I'd rather just watch for now." No one wants to make you feel uncomfortable.

Important to know: You can always say, "I pass," if asked to do anything that you don't want to do, like share or read aloud.

The selected readings usually last from five to ten minutes. Listen to them. This will tell you much about CMA and its philosophy.

Then sometime, either early or late in the meeting, the group observes what's called "the seventh tradition"—which states that all CMA groups must be self supporting. This is when a basket gets passed for donations. A dollar is plenty. Also, it's more than acceptable to just pass along the basket without putting in any money. Many people do. If you go to one or more meetings a day – sometimes people go to two or three – it can get too expensive to put a dollar in the basket each time. No one should judge you. This basket is also where you will drop your Court Cards or Sober House Cards, to be signed by the secretary, if you have these.

Fairly soon, within 15 minutes of the start of the meeting, you'll get to the speaker portion. At a meeting where the speaker has 30 minutes or more to talk, you'll often hear their whole recovery story—from what it used to be like in their using days, to what happened to make them quit, to what it's like for them now in recovery. The better meetings tend to focus more on the recovery side of our stories, but hearing the horror tales repeated every once in a while is a good reminder of how awful life was when using.

Some meetings only let the speaker share from 5 to 10 minutes. It just depends on the meeting. After the speaker finishes, the meeting is opened to general participation. That means you can raise your hand and the leader, usually, will call on a person to share. If you don't raise your hand, you don't have to speak. (The only exception is a "round robin" meeting, and these will be identified in the meeting schedule. In a round robin everyone, around the room, shares for a limited time. It's a good type of meeting to go to if you are shy and want to force yourself to share.) Most meetings have a 3-5 minute limit on sharing. Sometimes a person holds a timer, just in case.

At one point, usually about five minutes before the hour is up, the secretary of the meeting will call the sharing to an end, make a few announcements about housekeeping or CMA business, and then have someone lead the meeting out with the Serenity Prayer.

"God, grant me the serenity to accept the things I cannot change, the courage to change the things I can, and the wisdom to know the difference. Amen."

And the meeting is over. All in just under an hour.

But don't forget the "meeting after the meeting," where a group of people stand around and talk with one another. Often, some of the group go out for pizza or coffee. This is called "fellowship." It's a great way to get to better know the people in your CMA group.

Slogans, Slogans... and more Slogans

At just about any 12 Step meeting you'll hear them. Take it one day at a time... easy does it... stick with the winners... this too shall pass... meeting makers make it... what other people think of me is none of my business... and so on.

Oftentimes these slogans seem overly simplistic, like something designed for a bumper sticker instead of a serious recovery program. But here's the thing.

Like it or not, they generally offer some pretty good advice. I know it took me several months to stop resenting the robotic way people repeated these clichés at meetings. But eventually I began to hear the message beyond the slogan and I learned a lot.

So expect the slogans, but try to hear the deeper wisdom beneath the shallow surface of the bumper sticker. There's powerful truth in there.

Can I "Pass" If I'm Called On to Share?

Absolutely. Don't worry about having to share if you don't want to. If it's a "round robin" meeting or if you are called upon by the leader to share—which can sometimes happen if no one is volunteering—you can always respond, "I'm new and I think I'll pass for now." No one will judge you.

What About "Clean Time"?

A few meetings, definitely in the minority, ask that you state your clean time when you self-identify. This is to show the newcomer that it's possible to attain longtime sobriety. You'll hear people with a couple of years under their belts, some with 6 or more. If you have less than 30 days, you'll usually get applause for being present. Again, at CMA they remember how difficult are the first 30 days. (Getting your 30 day chip is a *really* big deal in CMA.) If you don't want to say how many clean days you have, you can always say, "I'm [name], a crystal meth addict, and I have today." This is fine, too. I know recovering addicts with years of sobriety who, when asked to state their clean time, always say, on principle, "I have today."

Again, usually, most meetings do not ask for you to state your clean time so it's not an issue.

What Are The "12 Steps" Anyway?

The 12 Steps are the core of any program based on the principles of the Alcoholics Anonymous. A lot has been written about the 12 Steps—literally, shelves of books—but all you need to understand here is that, at one point in any 12 Step recovery program, you will "work" through the steps with a sponsor (a fellow addict whose done them himself/herself).

They are posted on a sign in just about every meeting hall.

The steps have worked for hundreds of thousands, if not millions, of addicts since the 1930s. They can work for you, too. The main goal in completing the 12 Steps is to bring about a "personality" change that's powerful enough to transform your life of addiction into a life totally free from crystal meth. Honesty, open-mindedness, willingness are all that's required.

Know you don't have to start working the steps right away. Attend a few meetings. Get the feel for things. You'll know when it's time to find a sponsor to help you "work the steps." Until then, just keep an open mind and listen to what people share in the rooms about how the Steps are helping them stay clean.

How To Find "My" Meeting

You usually have one meeting that you consider your "home group," which is the meeting that's primary to your recovery, that you don't miss no matter what. Sometimes your home group is the first meeting you attend. Sometimes you'll try out many different meetings before you find just the right one.

Remember, "meeting makers make it." It's not unusual for a newcomer to attend at least one meeting a day.

The rule of thumb is to give a new meeting at least half a dozen tries before you decide one way or the other. Recovery experts believe it takes six meetings before you can accurately understand a group's particular dynamics and tone.

What if I Don't Like 12 Step Meetings?

There are other types of group meetings for people seeking recovery. The most common are those lead by a counselor/facilitator. Many of these, however, are part of an out-patient recovery program that you'll also be required to attend.

The best advice I can offer if you just don't like 12 step meetings is: keep coming back anyway. This is how you can make new sober friends. You don't have to get a sponsor and start working "the steps" in order to attend the meetings. As it says in the selected readings, the only requirement for membership in CMA is the desire to quit crystal meth. Period.

In summary...

Go, force yourself out of your comfort zone. Introduce yourself. Really, where else are you going to meet so many recovering tweakers?

Chapter 5

The Wall

6 Weeks – 4 Months

You hit it hard. All the positive, forward momentum from the Honeymoon crashes around you.

A seemingly insurmountable Wall of depression, boredom, and despair—it usually begins about 45 days into sobriety and it continues through month 4 or thereabouts. Rarely, however, does the Wall last longer than month 6. So, keep in mind, it's going to get better.

The Wall is often where people will relapse. You so want the feelings of boredom and loneliness to pass, crystal meth seems like the solution again. Though the danger of picking up is highest here, you can get past it.

Let's look at what to expect and what you can do to get through this stage of your recovery. The Wall is not impossible to overcome, just tricky.

It feels like hell. If life's going to be like this,
why not use?

— Tim, 3 months clean

Don't isolate. Call people.

— Billy, 1½ years clean

WHAT TO EXPECT

Exhaustion, Loneliness, and Boredom Return

You feel unfocused in life, bored by it all. Not only are you emotionally low, but you're physically spent. Instead of the energized life of the Honeymoon, you're overcome with exhaustion and sluggishness. You may feel intense bouts of loneliness.

This Wall is normal. Expect it. Know it's coming.

Usually, you begin to feel much better between months 4 to 6. So hang in there. You will indeed feel energetic and hopeful again. Don't let the boredom, loneliness, and sluggishness be an excuse to use. In fact, the Wall is the result of your brain and body healing. It's actually a sign that your brain is getting better. You need only keep moving forward, and not give in to your disease's temptation of escape.

What If I Don't Ever Feel Pleasure?

What if you feel no joy in life whatsoever? This profound inability to feel pleasure is a common consequence of prolonged meth use and usually begins about 1½ months after quitting. This can last through months 4 to 6. It's so common, in fact, there is a name for it—anhedonia.

It's tempting to say, "If this is how it's going to feel to be sober, I might as well use again. I certainly can't live this way forever." What you need to know is this temporary lack of pleasure is normal. Again, not only will it pass in a few months, it is actually a sign that *your brain is healing* and to be expected. Ride it out. Like the boredom and loneliness, your pleasure flatline won't last forever.

Using Fantasies, Flashbacks, and Euphoric Recall

In your using years, your body and brain get accustomed to high levels of stimulation. And once you hit the Wall, your brain is not a happy camper. It wants the fast-paced party back immediately. In short, your motto becomes: "I want more, now!" So what happens?

Your cravings for crystal return in full force. Thoughts of using or risky sexual fantasies can become obsessions. You want the rush of excitement crystal used to bring you. Anything to get past the boredom, loneliness, and depression.

The problem with these using fantasies and flashbacks is they are usually incomplete. It's called "euphoric recall." You recall only those exciting, fun and stimulating parts of using—and conveniently forget the overwhelmingly awful side of the experience. You recall half memories, at best.

Euphoric recall is the grand lie of your disease. It wants you only to remember the energy and excitement. Expect this lie—and don't be fooled. You know better. Recall the entire memory, down to the gritty, ugly end of your using days.

Sexual Appetite Spikes

"I want more, now!" translates into a spike in sexual appetite. If you've had relatively low sexual urges thus far, that will most likely change at some point during the Wall. Perhaps it's because the pleasure pathways of the brain aren't functioning and so you desperately want to jump start pleasure. Regardless of the emotional or biochemical reason behind this spike, your sexual appetite usually comes back with a vengeance.

Be careful. Many a recovering addict started using again because of sex. For gay men, it's the number one reason for relapse. I suspect the urge is just as strong for heterosexual couples, as well. (Of course, it is.)

Later in this chapter, we'll take a closer look at sex. (See "Goodbye Crystal Sex, Hello Sober Sex" at the end of this chapter.) For now, just know that, if it hasn't already, your sexual appetite is soon to spike.

Nerve Misfires or Jolts

On occasion, you may get a "jolt" through your body. It's the same kind of jolt you get just before you drift off into sleep and half-dream that you're falling over—and you jolt awake. In a wholly non-medical capacity, I call this a "nerve misfire."

I've seen recovering meth addicts start to sit in a chair and literally miss the chair because of a jolt. Don't be embarrassed. They are usually few and far between and will lessen, and eventually end, within a few months.

Getting an Earful from Friends and Family

Just when you are starting to recover somewhat and no longer feel like Frankenstein's monster, others notice your improvement and suddenly decide it's time to have that blunt conversation about your using. In short, you're just well enough to get dumped on by otherwise well-meaning friends and family.

Try not to bite their heads off.

If you can muster the patience, explain that you are not well enough to have this conversation. You know they care. But now is not the time for any deep, serious conversation about anything, especially your using.

Excuses and Justifications to Use Increase Ten-Fold

I can't emphasize it enough: it's in this period of your recovery where relapse is most common—and there is a reason. Your body is no longer producing the higher levels of dopamine that it did during the Pink Cloud. You've come up against a biochemical wall in your brain—and only time, because that's how the brain heals, can resolve this issue. But since your brain is screaming, "I want more, now," your disease jumps in with some grand excuses and justifications for why now is a good time to "use just a little bit" or "only once more" to alleviate the boredom and loneliness. Here are some of the disease's favorite relapse lies:

> *It's only for this one time.*
> *I've quit for three months, isn't it time I gave myself a little reward.*
> *If life is going to suck like this forever, I might as well use again.*
> *I can hangout with an old using buddy. If he uses in front of me, I'll just refuse.*
> *My hookup can use crystal because I'll be able to refuse.*
> *I'll go ahead since it's only for this one time.*
> *A little line for energy isn't the same as smoking or slamming.*
> *No one will know, so why not use again? Just this once?*

It's important to remember, you have one of the few diseases in the world that tries to convince you that you don't have it.

WHAT TO DO

Prioritize Meetings

According to recovery professionals, the main reasons that crystal meth addicts relapse are boredom and loneliness.

That means to keep from relapsing you need to: 1) keep busy and 2) keep the company of sober friends. Which translates, basically, into... you need to attend a lot of meetings. In AA they have a saying, "Meeting makers make it."

As you start getting better, it's easy to think, "I'm doing so well, I can cut back on my CMA (or AA) meetings and focus on other things." Beware of this kind of faulty thinking. Usually, when a little voice tells you to stop going to meetings that are helping you keep sober, it's your disease talking. The truth is: you need to keep busy, which means making room for all those meetings *first*.

The bottom line is you must put your recovery first, which for now means putting meetings first. It's the fellowship of your sober friends (who *really* understand you) that keeps you from being lonely. And it's attending a meeting a day, or more, that keeps you busy. This may seem like a lot, but it's only your life we're talking about here. And your life is worth the effort.

Let's say it again: meeting makers make it.

Keep Avoiding High-Risk People, Places, and Things

If you've not yet deleted all your old using contacts, or have kept some of those online accounts on hold instead of deleting them altogether, now is the time.

What are the high-risk people, places, or things in your life? Old using friends? Online communities? Dance clubs, sex clubs, or bars? Certain streets or parts of town? Certain movies or television shows that romanticize using?

There's another saying in AA that goes: *If you hang around a barbershop long enough, you're gonna get a haircut.*

Just because you've got a few months of sobriety under your belt doesn't mean you no longer have to avoid high-risk people, places, and things.

Exercise and the Gym

In this stage of your recovery it is vital to begin exercising regularly. Exercise is not only for your body's muscles. Meth's effects can be particularly long lasting and harmful to the brain. Studies by Harvard psychiatrist John Ratey, M.D., show that a fast-paced workout increases the production of specialized brain cells that affect learning and memory. He found that regular exercise not only relieves anxiety and mild to moderate depression, it literally *helps the brain heal faster*. And, just as importantly, a fast-paced workout actually helps redirect the brain away from cravings and fights off the impulse to use – often for hours. Important information to remember.

So, as a recovering meth addict you exercise for three reasons: 1) it's good for your body and overall well being; 2) it assists your brain in healing faster; and 3) it helps counteract the impulse to use.

Should you exercise? Duh.

One other scientific fact it helps to know: it takes 21 days for your brain to create a new habit. If you are at day 18 of exercising and you think, "This is useless and I hate it," stick with it through day 21 and, most likely, you'll feel differently.

Join a gym or an exercise class and give it at least 21 days. This is the new you in recovery.

Keep Busy – Declare War on Boredom

Boredom is the great enemy of sobriety. Start to keep a busy calendar. Set up coffee dates with as many of your non-using friends as possible. Go out to eat or to the movies. (If you're like most tweakers, you haven't been to a restaurant or movie in ages.) Keep yourself busy. Here are just a few good ideas:

Volunteer for a non-profit organization. This is the best because it not only fills the empty time in your day, but gives you a sense of doing something worthwhile and builds self-esteem.

Join an art class, or some kind of group activity that meets regularly.

Up the number of CMA or AA meetings you go to in a day. Take "commitments" at those meetings.

Go to the gym or take a yoga class.

Start a creative project—painting, writing, dancing, singing or whatever floats your boat creatively.

You get the picture. Keep yourself busy. Make plans and fill your calendar with commitments of one kind or another—and then keep those commitments. As the old saying goes, "An idle mind is the Devil's workshop." In this case, it's very true. So declare war on boredom and inactivity.

Schedule Medical and Dental Checkups

In the first year of your recovery, see your doctor every three months to update him or her on your progress. Be sure he or she knows you were a meth addict and the truthful extent of how much and how long you used. Only in this way will your physician be able to make sure you get the proper care you need. Make your doctor an important part of your sobriety team.

If you were negative for HIV and Hep C, get tested again several months into your sobriety.

If you haven't yet scheduled that dental exam, do so now.

Collect Milestone Chips at Meetings

At CMA or NA meetings they give chips for various lengths of sobriety. There's a "welcome chip," often called the "24 hour chip," then a 30, 60 and 90 day chip. Then comes the 6 month chip, the 9 month chip, and another big one—your first birthday in sobriety—the 1 year chip.

The reason it's important to take these chips publicly is two-fold. First, it's important to honor your sobriety for yourself and your friends. And, second—and maybe this is even more important—it's important to show the newcomer who's only got a few days that, yes, it's possible to quit crystal meth.

Remember when you were the newcomer with only a few weeks of sobriety under your belt? Remember how amazed you were to watch others take their 30 day or 6 month chip?

Those chip-takers at meetings weren't just taking their milestone chips for themselves. They were taking it for the newcomer, you. Now that you're no longer a newcomer, you can return the favor.

Safety in Numbers

It's true and you know it is. Hang around sober people. Hang around recovering addicts like yourself. Also don't live your sober life in the closet. Of course, not everyone in your life needs to know you were a crystal meth addict, but a significant number of your closest friends should know. You need people who will support you in your sobriety, not enable you in denying your addiction.

If a friend doesn't know you are a recovering addict, they are much more likely to accidentally enable bad behavior. To your closest friends, come out of the recovering addict closet. It'll make you closer.

Goodbye Crystal Sex, Hello Sober Sex

If you combined sex and crystal, sober sex might seem overwhelming at first. But thousands of recovering tweakers have relearned how to have healthy— even hot—sex without crystal. It's just going to take some time and effort.

Though, this could just as easily be placed in the "Adjustment" phase of your recovery (the next chapter), a brief "how to" on sober sex is included here because it's during this stage of your recovery that the sexual desires often come roaring back in the form of fantasies or cravings. Anything to escape the boredom, right?

First, the harsh fact: *no more crystal sex ever.* Why? Because having crystal sex means putting crystal into your body one more time—and that you can't risk. The reality is there's no such thing as a one-night stand when it comes to crystal. It comes for days, then might not leave for years. You can't afford to take this risk.

Life without meth means life without meth-fueled sex. It's okay, even necessary for some, to mourn this loss.

One complaint you hear a lot from former tweakers is: regular sex seems dull and just doesn't feel as good as it did on crystal. There's a physiological reason for this. After all the repeated and intense dopamine dumps in your brain, the fibers in the pathway associated with sex are damaged. But just as with most other pleasurable feelings, this will change over time. Your brain will heal and you'll definitely start enjoying sex again. Just remember it takes time and effort on your part.

Also, sober sex is a different kind of sex. Instead of the limit-pushing, intense, compulsive, nonstop-pleasure marathons you used to have on crystal, you'll have normal sex. If this sounds boring to you, it's just because you're still operating from the perspective of meth-fueled sex.

Imagine charting your pleasure on a scale of 1 to 10. If you think back to your *first* orgasm, whether having sex with another person or masturbating, it was probably so intense and amazing that it scored off the charts—say, a 15. But, after a few more sexual experiences, each orgasm no longer felt so new and intense. Orgasm leveled off to where it belonged, near the top of the "normal" pleasure scale, close to 10.

Like that first orgasm, the first time you had sex on crystal was off the charts. But it was much higher than a 15 because it created an unnatural physiological state that the human brain could never reach on its own. In short, that first experience of crystal sex was closer to a 60. By comparison, sober sex quickly became unsatisfying. After repeated experiences with 60-level crystal sex, regular sex felt empty and boring and on the 1 to 10 scale, sober sex probably rated a 3 or less.

It's important to remember this 3 manifests from the distorted perspective of crystal meth—an expectation of 60-level pleasure that the human brain *was never meant to experience*. After quitting meth, regular sober sex may continue to feel like a 3 or less for awhile. However, in time, your perspective returns to normal and sober sex begins to feel enjoyable again. Of course, sober sex will never be as intense as that 60 of crystal sex, but it will again become one of your great pleasures in life.

Your brain adjusts. Trust the thousands of meth addicts who successfully quit before you—the 10 of natural sex will not only be "enough" but amazing in its own right, just as it was intended to be.

So how do you handle sex in sobriety? There is only one rule: no crystal sex. Here are some ideas…

Wait a year. I've heard it said in CMA that, if you are not already in a relationship, it's healthy to stay away from sex for a full year. This gives you time to work on your recovery without the complications of a major trigger.

Don't wait, but keep it sober. On the other hand, in the early days of CMA, it was sometimes suggested that newcomers have sex with members who had some sobriety under their belt—a big "no-no" in AA circles. The rationale was that, if you have sober sex with a newcomer, at least they're learning to have sober sex and are less likely to relapse with crystal sex. (These were mostly gay male meetings in Los Angeles.)

Regardless, you will mourn the loss of crystal sex. In *Overcoming Crystal Meth Addiction*, Steven J. Lee, M.D., a psychiatrist who specializes in addiction, uses the analogy of a "trip to Antarctica with breathtaking sunrises over colossal glistening snow peaks, unlike anything you could see on this planet" as a way to put the loss of crystal sex into perspective. On the expedition to Antarctica, you face tremendous challenges. Your body and soul take a beating—it's 20 degrees below zero with fifty-mile-per-hour winds and you get dangerously lost for awhile along the way.

But after this long, difficult and very costly journey, you get to experience something few people ever do: the unseen world of Antarctica. Then, like Dorothy in Kansas, the journey is over and you find yourself back home in the normal, everyday world. But you have an amazing memory to carry with you for the rest of your life. Lee writes, "the immense physical effort and financial cost to get there remind you that this is a place not meant for humans to see. That makes the memory that much more precious—the realization that you saw the unseeable."

Once more: unlike most people in the world, you actually experienced Antarctica and still have amazing memories of the journey. But you'll never go back. *Those once-in-a-lifetime peak experiences are over.* "This is an important admission you need to make to yourself," Lee continues, "because any hidden fantasy that one day you will have crystal sex again is a seed that can grow into an uncontrollable craving and a relapse."

You'll have to grieve the loss and accept it—or else risk relapse.

Remember the stages of grieving: denial, anger, bargaining, depression, and, finally, acceptance. These are applicable to your grief over losing crystal sex forever. *Denial:* I don't have to think of "not-having crystal sex" as a forever thing. *Anger:* I want to have that experience again, damn it. *Bargaining:* I can have crystal sex for one night a month, right? *Depression:* No, I can't because crystal doesn't do one-night stands. *Acceptance:* Since I don't want crystal to ruin my life, I'll have to give up crystal sex forever, which is a worthy exchange.

Sex is tricky. And that's the understatement of the year. There's only one thing that's certain: a healthy and active sex life is important to happiness.

So given that, here are three final points to consider about sober sex:

You were emotionally connected to the meth-fueled sex, not to the other person. It's a lie that you were "more connected" to your sex partner while using meth. Though you might have been *physically* connected while having a wild party, it was actually the meth and sex that you were *emotionally* connected to, not the person. Be honest, your sex partner could have been almost anyone. The meth was the crucial element. In sober sex, you have the opportunity to experience a genuine emotional connection with another person—something you didn't get with crystal.

After you get comfortable with sober sex, you will be able to have those 10-level experiences again and, most importantly, that will be enough. It's true. And don't fall into the trap of thinking normal sex is just a weaker, tamer version of that wild beast crystal sex. Because the truth is that sober sex is a *different animal* altogether. Sober sex has its own rewards of intense pleasure that sex on meth will never have. Remember kissing? Remember going slowly, and feeling that warm glow from happiness you felt as you explored your partner? Remember feeling really connected, looking your partner in the eyes and staring deep into their being? Even though you'll always have your memories of crystal sex, the intense desire to have it again will pass with time. You may have flashbacks and intense memories from time to time, but they will lessen.

What you get to have in sobriety are sober experiences—and that includes sex. Relearning how to have sober sex could be a book in itself. The main tenets are: *don't use no matter what and give yourself permission to change.* Other than using, if you want, you can try everything you did while thwacked out on crystal. But, today, you get to try it sober. Then, if you find that certain sexual practices don't work for you anymore, you can, in a sober and respectful way, change those practices.

Sobriety is not about making our past behavior wrong. Other than using, it's fair game to experiment with your experience—give it a try sober. You may like it. Or you may feel that certain attitudes toward sex no longer work for the sober you. It's not uncommon for the "no strings attached" sexploits of a person's using days suddenly to seem empty and hollow because, in sobriety, you now want something more meaningful—a "connection" to another person beyond NSA. If this happens to you, then, in a sober and respectful way, begin looking for more lasting connections.

Sex does again become a peak experience. It's just that now it's a 10 at best. Now, it's what is humanly possible. Sex could be fabulous enough before crystal. It will be again afterwards, too.

Chapter 6

Adjustment

4 – 6 Months

You've gotten over the Wall safely and it is now mostly behind you. The next stage is called "Adjustment" because that's what characterizes this time period—adjusting, physically, socially, and emotionally, to life without crystal. You get relief from the overwhelming cravings and begin to find life interesting again.

It doesn't have to get any worse. Your life will get better. One day, you'll find yourself laughing and happy again. Promise.

— Joseph, 1 year clean

Surround yourself with lots of clean time, with people who've been clean for awhile.

— Nicki, 22 years clean

WHAT TO EXPECT

Getting Better Through the Rough Patches

As you progress into the first year, your brain will become sharper and more focused. Life becomes manageable again and everything may seem very new. You definitely feel yourself getting better. The heightened emotions, mood swings, and memory loss that persisted for the first few months of recovery are fading, but it's to be expected that you'll still encounter some rough patches.

Try to ride out those rough patches, because no matter how you look at it, your life is definitely trending toward the positive now that you're clean and sober. Keep an eye on the bigger picture, keep an eye on your life's improvement since you quit.

Your life is getting better. Just slowly. And with some rough patches.

Triggers & Cravings Lessen

With time, triggers and cravings generally lessen. Most recovering addicts have fewer cravings as the months add up. Excluding rough patches where everything is more extreme, triggers may happen only every few weeks or so. What used to be a daily occurrence often becomes a weekly occurrence.

First-Time Sober Experiences

Now that you're not using, you get to have—or have again—various "first-time" sober experiences. From sex to holidays to your child's birthday, there are a lot of very important experiences that you now get to have sober, either for the first time or "again" for the first time. I personally believe each renewed first is to be celebrated as a big deal—because it is. Most likely, you thought you'd never again enjoy some of life's simple pleasures free of crystal. But today, a new world free of meth's bondage literally opens before you.

The process works like this:

You do some action or experience—let's say, for example, sex—and do it sober. After you have the experience, you get to decide if you liked it or not. You make an adult choice and choose if you want to have that experience again in the same way or, perhaps, change it up a bit. Sex is interesting to discuss because, quite often, what worked for us sexually while high, doesn't work so well sober. We're just not in that "dark" place and, certainly, sex doesn't last for five hours anymore. But let's suppose you have your first sober sexual experience and, on reflection, it doesn't "feel right" to you. There's no blame, here. You didn't do something you shouldn't have—as long as you were sober and didn't harm anyone else, it's okay. Sobriety is about finding out who you are again without meth or other drugs in your system. And only one thing is certain: you are a different person now that you're sober.

Without a doubt, many experiences are now going to feel different.

Some of these first-time experiences you'll not recognize until after you've done them. One recovering addict told me she'd forgotten, until she did it again sober, how much she loved to shop every Saturday at the local farmer's market. Again, I like to think of all these experiences as first-time events even if they are not. Because they are all "firsts" as far as your new sober life is concerned.

Pay attention to your new milestone moments. Mother's Day, Father's Day, Christmas, Hanukkah, New Year's Eve, a birth in your family, the first funeral you are able to show up for sober. These are the obvious big moments. But don't forget the little events. The trip to the farmer's market, or your first crisp autumn morning or balmy summer night. These new first-time experiences are a big deal. So celebrate them. That's a big deal.

If you are like me, you never thought you'd get to live life sober again. Life without this awful drug in your body—what an amazing thing to experience all over again for the first time.

Weight Gain

At the beginning of our recovery, weight gain is all good. In the harsh light of sobriety, that "heroin chic" look you'd fashioned wasn't so pretty, despite what your disease kept telling you. Try to embrace your weight gain.

But what about *excessive* weight gain later on in your recovery? One addict said to me, "Now that I've quit meth for a year, I'm 40 pounds heavier than before I started using." The best solution to unwanted weight gain (and what a problem to have compared to meth addiction) is to increase the rate of your metabolism. At this point, consulting a nutritionist would be a good idea.

But for those who don't go the nutritionist route, for whatever reason, here are some simple ways to increase your rate of metabolism. Try eating 5 smaller meals a day, instead of the usual 3 or 2 large ones. Increase your water intake—a lot. It's probably safe to say you could just double the amount of water you drink now. Also caffeinated drinks actually dehydrate you and so don't count. And neither do sodas, we're talking water, period. Eat healthy fresh foods, not frozen. And, finally, this is crucial: exercise daily. Yes, the best advice to rid yourself of unwanted excessive weight is good old-fashioned moderation of calorie intake and regular exercise.

Sleep Normalizes, Kinda

Usually, sometime in the first year, sleep normalizes. For some it's as early as month 2, but for others it can take much of the year. Of course, if you're pre-disposed genetically to sleep problems, you'll have a harder time. I still take Benadryl every night, but insomnia runs in my family.

Eventually, sleep normalizes. *Kinda.*

Sexual Urges Normalize, Kinda

Or, to put it another way, the extreme sexual urges you had during the Wall begin to lessen. Sex is just such a big, messy deal for many of us—it was for me—that it's a relief when this aspect of your sobriety begins to normalize. If it's taking you longer than 6-12 months, let me say: I understand and it's okay.

It took me well into this stage of my recovery before I could begin reintegrating sex into my sober life. But it does happen.

Your sexual urges do begin to normalize. *Kinda.*

Past Feelings Are Going to "Complete" Themselves

As you journey through the first year, you also begin to realize much of what you've lost because of your crystal addiction—the lost friendships and opportunities, the years of life gone forever. This realization sometimes comes with sadness, as we grieve what could have been, especially had meth not ruled our lives for so long a time. This is all a way of saying, there's a lot of grief for loss that occurs during your first year. Probably, you are going to have or experience some intense feelings.

This should be expected and know you are not backsliding in your recovery. You are actually beginning to experience emotions that your meth use repressed. Ultimately, it's a good thing.

Feelings have a beginning, a middle, and an end. During your drug years, you didn't fully experience those feelings. You bypassed them with an emotional high from using. So whatever powerful emotions that were stirred in you—from the death of a parent, the break up of a relationship, the loss of a job or friendship, any powerful emotion from anger to fear to grief—were not completely felt. So it's now, during your first year, that all those incomplete feelings will need to "complete" themselves.

Consequences from the Damages Done While Using

It's also during this Adjustment that you begin to realize the extent of the damages done by your crystal addiction—the destroyed relationships, the squandered and missed opportunities, the pain you caused others. This realization often comes with great remorse. But the flip side is you can actually see clearly now. And now that you can see the consequences from the damages done while using, you can begin to make these right and, definitely, not repeat them.

Again you are faced with completing emotions you would not fully felt and grieving over what you've lost, but there is also a sense of growing hope. Overall, you have to admit: *it's getting better.*

You are looking at your life's larger picture for the first time in a good long while—and beginning to take responsibility. You are beginning to show up for others in life who count on you.

WHAT TO DO

When You Don't Want to Avoid a Trigger: Feel It and Move Through It

The advice to avoid obvious triggers is especially good in the early weeks and months, but the ultimate goal is to be able to handle—to feel and move through—any trigger which comes your way. You can't simply avoid triggers forever. So let's look at an example of a trigger you know is coming—and how you might cope with it.

Suppose large family gatherings usually trigger you. In the past, you've always responded to the pressure of such situations by using. But now that you are clean and sober, there will be family gatherings where you'll need to show up without getting loaded. Let's take an obvious example, a funeral. You'll want to be responsible and support your family. So, how do you handle this triggering situation?

You handle it exactly the same as you would any sudden trigger. You lean on a sober friend.

Instead of calling someone or going to a CMA meeting, you ask your sober friend beforehand to accompany you to the family gathering. If you get a craving, you'll have your sober friend there by your side. You can literally lean on them, if needed.

Knowing you are likely to be triggered, you don't run away. Instead, you prepare ahead of time. You are able to feel the trigger and have your support system in place so you can move through it. There's an old saying that goes: *feel the fear and do it anyway*. It's like that with a trigger you know you must eventually face, better awkward than backward.

As you grow in your sobriety you will become stronger and more able to handle the triggers that life throws at you. You'll prepare by having tools at your disposal—CMA meetings in which to share, sober friends on whom to lean—that help you become the person of character you want to become.

Go Back to Work or School

I'll say it again: according to recovery professionals, the main reasons crystal meth addicts relapse are boredom and loneliness. So go back to work or school as soon as you can without stressing yourself out too much. It's a balance.

Work With a Therapist

If you haven't already begun to, now is definitely the time to begin working with a therapist, as opposed to a drug counselor alone. You have moved from early abstinence, where the problems encountered were mostly physical and about learning to live without crystal, into a more solid recovery—where the problems you face are mostly emotional and personal.

Meth gave you an instant way to escape emotional distress. One hit and nothing else mattered. All worries vanished, problems dissolved. Using meth "changed the channel" from distress to immense pleasure—instantly. The problem you face today in sobriety is how to deal with the painful feelings you formerly escaped by using. How do you cope with emotional distress now that you no longer use? This is a question all good therapists address with their patients.

The truth many therapists working with addicts have come to realize is: the traditional "talk therapy" model that explores the emotional conflicts of childhood has its limitations. Though this form of therapy might be comforting, it rarely brings about an *actual change* in adult behavior. Insight into past experiences can validate the pain you yearn to escape, but it doesn't offer any practical way to change the old, bad behaviors that currently lead to unhappiness and using. In order to change old behaviors, the addict *needs to learn and practice new life skills* that reinforce a whole new set of behaviors.

Psychotherapy focusing on learning these new behaviors is becoming more common in treatment programs today. These therapies include dialectical behavior therapy, acceptance and commitment therapy, and cognitive behavior therapy. I recommend you find a therapist who specializes in one of these—though, finally, a good therapist is one who imparts skills that actually make a difference in their patients' lives, no matter what form of therapy is practiced.

If you can't afford to see a therapist or don't have insurance that covers therapy, check out local nonprofit organizations to discover what kinds of free mental health services might be available in your area. In Los Angeles, there are several weekly group therapy meetings specifically for recovering crystal meth addicts that are offered at minimal or no cost. Your options are greater in a large metropolitan area, but you never know what your local university or hospital might have to offer until you check for yourself.

Keep Vigilant about Sex Without Crystal

Sex takes many of us back out. Boredom and loneliness, remember. Sex falls into the loneliness category. I mention sex again because it's such an overwhelmingly huge issue for many of us recovering tweakers. And it's an issue that doesn't go away.

Here are some things for you to consider when keeping vigilant about sex without crystal:

If your sex partner has very little time in sobriety, be extra careful. They are much closer to their using days and still have powerful associations between using and sex. When it comes to recovery from crystal meth, it's often the newcomer to sobriety that is most predatory—just because they are more likely to use the drug for seduction.

Also, what about people from your using past who are now in recovery? A good rule of thumb is: if you ever had crystal sex with a person, you shouldn't try to have sober sex with them because it's just too reminiscent of that particular sex-high. You are likely to get triggered.

For most addicts I know who associated using with sex, there's nothing more difficult than navigating sexual issues. It's an ongoing concern. Work with a counselor or therapist. Seek out new venues in which to find sex partners that are sober—like an AA or CMA meeting, not to mention sober conventions. Some cities have "sober coffeehouses" that cater specifically to those in recovery.

Now might be a good time to reread the earlier section "Goodbye Crystal Sex, Hello Sober Sex" in Chapter 5.

Make Plans and Keep a Socially Active Calendar

At many rehab centers, clients begin their week by making a detailed, hour by hour, plan of what they wish to accomplish for the following week. They list all 12 Step meetings, gym visits, therapy and doctor's appointments, housekeeping times, along with meals, and any social dates—everything—and get it down on paper. This becomes a kind of a contractual agreement between yourself and the universe. You keep to this busy plan no matter what. Your sobriety depends upon it.

There are two aspects to this accomplishment list. First, you have busily scheduled yourself so that there are not many consecutive hours in any given day that are free—no time to get bored. And, second, you have written it all down so you can consult it from time to time—you have a definite plan. I think this is a good practice to do every Sunday evening. Make out your detailed plan for the following week. If you have any large chunks of free time in any of the days, find something to schedule there instead. Call your sober friends and make fellowship dates—to see a movie or go shopping, to have coffee or hike a trail. Anything will work, as long as it involves being socially active with other sober individuals. But fill up that calendar.

It seems simple because it is. Keep a busy schedule and keep socially active. Make plans to do so and follow those plans. Do this and your temptation to use will be minimized.

Chapter 7

Ongoing Recovery

6 – 12 Months

Toward the end of the first year clean, crystal meth addiction can seem distant and almost tangential to your life. Or, it can be something you continue to think about, fleetingly, almost every day. Like all things on this timeline, it depends.

I like to call this part of the quitting journey "Ongoing Recovery" (also known as the "Resolution" stage) because, despite how foreign your crystal dependence may seem, it's important to remember that meth addiction is a "chronic disease" and you are never cured.

Recovery is always ongoing.

It took me fifteen years and eight tries,
and it still wasn't until the pain of using
exceeded the pain of not using that I finally
surrendered.

— Steve, 4 years clean

WHAT TO EXPECT

Triggers and Cravings Out of Nowhere

Yes, this still happens. Just not as often. Perhaps you are no longer triggered by the songs you listened to while using, no longer triggered when driving through the neighborhood where your dealer lived, or by money to spend on payday. Time has worn the edges down and meth's reminders are not so prickly. For whatever reason, you just aren't triggered nearly as often as you were in early sobriety. You haven't had to use the techniques of "thought stopping" and "playing it forward" for weeks at a time, maybe even months.

Still, it will happen. Out of nowhere, you're triggered and find yourself fantasizing about getting high and you're glamorizing the ritual of how you used, remembering only the euphoric bliss of the rush.

You are not backsliding. It might be difficult to remember, but you are still less than a year clean. It takes a solid 2 years for the brain to heal completely from meth use. You're not halfway there. Cut yourself some slack and, when you have cravings, use the tools at your disposal. Stop the thought before it goes further. Or play that tape all the way through to the gritty, disgusting last day of your final run.

And then go to the gym to get some strenuous exercise. You know what to do.

Well Deserved Pride

I hope you feel some pride in what you've accomplished so far in your recovery. Getting clean of crystal meth is no easy feat. It takes persistence, courage, and strength. At your next CMA meeting, when you self-identify as "I'm a crystal meth addict," feel some well deserved pride in yourself. You've taken your life back. And those of us who are also on the recovery journey know just how difficult it's been.

Even though life may still be a struggle some days, take some pride in what you've accomplished—over half a year clean.

A year is just around the corner. One day at a time, of course.

And Still, My Disease Whispers Its Favorite Relapse Lies

Just because you've got some sober time doesn't mean your disease has gotten any less clever. Your disease is a master at manipulation and will eagerly use your recovery time against you. Here are just a few of its favorite relapse lies:

Partying for one night is not a real relapse.

It's been over six months now. You deserve a night off.

Snorting a line to get this project finished is not the same as partying.

You've proven that you can stop whenever you want. You've got control now.

What's the use of racking up all this clean time, if you're not going to celebrate with a party every once in a while?

You can recover on Sunday and be ready for work on Monday. No problem.

You're going to be out of town, away from your sober friends and family all week. Isn't it the perfect time to take a little party break?

It's not real using as long as you don't slam again. Smoking or snorting isn't nearly as serious.

Of course, you can have a drink. It won't end up with a drunken phone call to your dealer. You're an addict, not an alcoholic.

You get the idea. Remember, just because you've got some time under your belt doesn't mean your disease doesn't still want to kill you. It does.

WHAT TO DO

Put Recovery First

After half a year of sobriety, when life gets busy and full, it's tempting to let your recovery take a backseat. That's a big mistake. Don't forget you have one of the few diseases in the world that tells you, repeatedly, that you don't have it.

One sober living house I'm familiar with here in Palm Springs has each resident answer the following question at their daily check-in each evening: *What did I do today to put my recovery first?* If there's not much on the list, you don't get shamed, but asked to question deeper. Where's the room for improvement? What can you do tomorrow to put your recovery first? I think this is an excellent part of any daily review. Every evening, before you go to sleep, review the day and ask yourself when you put your recovery first. Also, be fearless about looking at when you put your recovery on the backburner. Did you miss a 12 Step meeting for a sporting event on TV? Did you skip your daily meditation because you were running late? Did you blow off the gym? (*Daily exercise is an important part of your recovery, remember?*) Again, the goal is not to shame yourself, but to improve your daily routine and practices so that your recovery is strengthened.

Now, as you move into the second half of your first year, it's more tempting than ever to forget that crucial principle of staying sober: *Always put your recovery first!*

Your disease will be whispering other suggestions nonstop. Don't listen. Put recovery first. Especially now that you're getting better.

Get to Know Yourself Again – the "New" Old You

This is an amazing time, often difficult. but always so beautiful because you are not using, because life is becoming more manageable. These first few months to a year are when you get to know yourself again. The real and authentic you had been hijacked by your addiction. You may have even forgotten what life was *like* before you started using. Maybe the life of an addict is all you've known. Or maybe you remember clearly those days before everything went to hell and meth ruled your life. Either way, you are now beginning to know yourself sober.

You have a choice. You'll either take the opportunity to explore yourself while sober, or will avoid personal growth altogether. I hope you choose exploration because getting to know the new and sober you is the best way to strengthen sobriety and stave off relapse.

There are many different ways to go about this "self actualization" route to better knowing yourself. From doing the 12 Steps to traditional psychotherapy, from Native American vision quests to theater games, there are many different and valid ways to explore your growing self. You'll find your own ways.

Later in the first year comes the beginnings of self reflection and the willingness to grow. And if you're not there yet, relax and don't worry. Your moments of extended serenity will increase over time as you get to know the "new" old you and you'll find a program of self-exploration and growth that works for you.

Volunteer

It's good to keep busy. One good way to fill your time with rewarding acts is to volunteer for a local nonprofit organization. From an urban LGBT center to a rural animal shelter, there are many great organizations that could use your time and energy. In just about every larger city and many smaller ones, as well, there's a rehab or recovery center where you can volunteer.

Also, you'll meet other sober people—not many drug addicts do volunteer work—and do some good in your community.

Throw a Birthday Party for My First Year

It may seem obvious, but I'm going to say it anyway. Throw yourself a big birthday bash when you turn "1" in your sobriety. It is an important milestone.

Receive a cake at your CMA or AA home group meeting.

Take a 1 year chip at every meeting you go to for a week following your birthday. Remember, you are taking these chips not only for yourself, but to show the newcomer and those with less time that long-term sobriety is possible.

Chapter 8

A Year and Beyond

Issues and concerns change as you move into multiple years of sobriety. This is a broad overview of a year and beyond...

You just stop. As you stay clean longer, you realize it's *your* choice as an individual as to whether or not you use.

—Jay, 5 years clean

Fear keeps me clean. I'm not afraid of dying. Most addicts aren't. I'm afraid of relapsing… and not making it back. I'm afraid I'll have a stroke and then my sister, who I don't like, will have to wipe my ass while I lie in bed, unable to move, for the rest of my life. That's the fear that keeps me sober today.

— Brian, 13 years clean

WHAT TO EXPECT

2 Years – the Brain's Magic Number

As you move into the second year, life often becomes manageable again and everything seems fresh and new. Your sleep returns to normal, or to whatever is normal for you. You go months and months without having a using dream.

Sometime near the end of your second year, most recovering addicts report they no longer have the mood swings or bouts of strong emotion they experienced in their early sobriety. The probable reason for this is that it takes about two years for the brain to heal from meth addiction. According to medical studies, two years is the magic number wherein the brain rebuilds itself to compensate for the damage done by meth.

This is not to say years 2 and 3 are going to be a breeze—read on. But when it comes to what to expect *physically*, usually they are much easier.

Floundering – A Few Years Into Sobriety

Once into year 3 or thereabouts, many recovering meth addicts report a period of floundering. Several people interviewed for this book stated unequivocally that years 3 and 4 were the hardest. You have gone through the pain and effort to attain physical sobriety and now are left with—yourself.

After the first year is when the work to attain "emotional sobriety" begins in earnest, when a deeper, exploratory psychotherapy with a traditional therapist (not a drug counselor) is often called for. If you've not yet begun to do so, this is when you explore all those emotions and feelings you were stuffing or hiding with your addiction.

This is also when, if you are in CMA or AA, it's important to be working with other addicts who have less time than you. Ask anyone who's been a "sponsor" and they'll say, when it comes to strengthening your own recovery, there's nothing like working with another addict. When you work with another addict, you take back that much more power from your disease and find yourself floundering less.

And a reminder about individuality. Several of the recovering addicts interviewed for this book encountered their period of floundering much later, in years 5 or 6. As with anything you read in this book, the timeline for you might vary considerably. There's only one you.

The point is to expect the period of floundering. It's normal. This is when it's very helpful to talk to someone who has more time than you.

Get their advice on how to move forward or, at the least, wait it out. This period of floundering will eventually pass. As always, the key is not to let the boredom and irritability serve as an excuse to use again.

Triggers and Cravings Mostly Disappear

Yes, this really happens. It's common for people with more than five years of sobriety to say, honestly, that they no longer have using thoughts or cravings. Triggers almost never arise. This seems to be the norm. About five years and you are a different person. Every seven years the entire human body is completely new—every cell has been replaced—so it makes sense that as you near the seven year mark, the old physical cravings would begin to leave.

Long-Term Consequences from Using

One of the big things you get to face in longtime sobriety is the consequences from the damages done while using. A 12 Step program deals with this aspect of your recovery like no other I know. It's why I suggest every addict do the 12 Steps at least once. It makes you look at the consequences from your time of using—and, most importantly, puts you into a process of making amends for those damages whenever possible.

If you can't make amends to the particular person or institution you damaged, you can at least fully acknowledge the carnage at your hand while in the thick of your disease. This needs to be done to further bolster your resolve to stay in recovery no matter what.

WHAT TO DO

Keep Moving – The Escalator Model

Imagine your addiction as an escalator that is constantly moving downward. You stand in the middle of the addiction escalator and what happens? If you don't move your feet, and start walking upward, the rolling staircase will take you lower into the depths of your illness. The moving steps are always downward. You must walk, sometimes run, up the steps just to remain in place. Otherwise the addiction escalator brings you down once again.

Climbing the escalator is the effort you put into your recovery. Eventually, as time passes and you have more sobriety under your belt, the escalator gets easier to climb and slower. As you climb, you move higher up in life, rather than continually walking just to stay in the same place. The lesson of this model is: you can't stop climbing because the escalator is always moving. If you stop climbing—meaning, you forget that you have a chronic illness that can never be cured and, as a result, no longer put your recovery first—the escalator will bring you back down into the depths of your addiction.

The escalator model is good to keep in mind as you get more time—after years, it's an easier climb and less difficult to maintain your current position—but you still can't afford to stop climbing altogether. You are only moving forward or you're moving backwards into the depths of your addiction. If you've been around recovery for a long time you may have heard it expressed like this: *We either grow or we go.*

You have a chronic illness that cannot be cured, but only treated. And treatment involves walking up the escalator, always. You must keep moving.

Don't Use No Matter What

This is the mantra of longtime sobriety. Of course, the problem is that it's just that—a saying. And when in the clutches of an overpowering craving it's probably not going to be enough. But adopted as your life's motto *and added to the other strategies and skills of recovery* you learn, this simple little saying can take on a powerful significance.

And, remember, don't use no matter what.

Deepen Spiritual Life

Though scientists estimate that genetic factors account for between 40 and 60 percent of a person's vulnerability to addiction, there's a part of our disease that we can't explain physiologically. A lot a research has been done into the psychological and environmental factors of addiction and, certainly, these are significant. What we're left with, at the end of the day, however, is a sneaking suspicion that addiction is a disease of the spirit, as well as the body.

Longtime recovery almost always entails a deepening of the spiritual life. And, here, I mean a broadly conceived notion of "spiritual life." It may not even entail a belief in God, *per se*. And you certainly don't need to be religious to be spiritual.

Explore. If you are working a 12 Step program then you are already involved in a spiritual program. If you are meditating, ditto. I can't tell you where to find it. I know one tweaker with over 15 years sobriety who honestly says his religion is Jedi—and he credits this Higher Power for his sobriety. It definitely works for him and I don't know a person who's sobriety I respect more than this man's. The truth is there are as many ways to explore spirituality as there are individuals.

Bottom line: the evidence seems to suggest that an evolving spiritual life is one of the cofactors in longtime sobriety.

Give Back – Pay It Forward

Another hallmark of longtime sobriety is the notion of giving back to other addicts who are still suffering. The programs of AA, NA, and CMA are particularly insistent on this as a method to stay clean and sober. After a year or so of sobriety, you are expected to become a "sponsor" and actively help others who have less sobriety than you.

But there are many ways to pay it forward.

More than a few recovering addicts have become specialists in the recovery field, actually going back to school in order to have a new career. In fact, most people you meet who work in recovery are recovering addicts of some sort—or have been touched personally by addiction in some profound way.

You could also do volunteer work for a particularly worthwhile charity. Or, if you are an artist, create a work about addiction and recovery. One of my ways of paying it forward is by writing this book. It's very literally part of my recovery process.

There are many ways to give back to life the gift you've received—a second chance, life in sobriety. The key is to give back. To pay it forward.

Chapter 9

What About Relapse?

We don't blame someone with high blood pressure or asthma for the biological malfunction happening in their bodies. And we certainly don't shame them when they have acute flare-ups of their illness. Why is it different for the meth addict? And what is relapse but an acute flare-up of your addiction/illness?

It's important to begin to understand addiction through the medical model so we can jettison the guilt and shame associated with relapses. This is not to excuse or encourage slips, but to be realistic. The fact is that many recovering meth addicts will slip during the journey of their recovery. I slipped and used several times before I finally quit. It's part of many of our stories. The goal for you, here, is to keep that slippage to a minimum.

In this chapter, we look at what to expect when you slip and how to minimize the duration of the relapse and, hopefully, not slip again.

Get help. Get out of guilt. Don't judge
yourself or beat yourself up. The past is past.

— Nolan, 9 months clean

WHAT TO EXPECT

Lie #1: Relapse is a Moral Failure

The statistics aren't pretty. One well-publicized estimate puts relapse rates at 92%. (Rehab centers have countered with their own statistics of meth users who successfully complete rehab – at a 10 to 30% relapse rate.) The statistic that rings true to my experience is one I've heard from several recovery professionals: a crystal meth addict will slip or relapse on average between 7 and 13 times before, finally, quitting.

But what does all this mean for you? First, the good news is you don't have to be average.

You can be the exception. This most recent relapse can be your last.

The key is to: 1) end your relapse as soon as possible, and 2) learn from it so it won't happen again. We'll look at this in greater detail shortly.

The truth. Recovering from crystal meth is a life-long challenge and very few people who are addicted stop using successfully the first time around. I'll say it again: the average is 7 to 13 relapses before success in quitting takes hold.

For most people, learning how to keep off meth is the same as learning a new skill—like riding a bicycle. Do you know many people who learned to ride a bicycle without falling over a few times? And some of us fell many times before we finally learned the skill.

Relapse does not mean moral failure. It is part of recovery for most addicts. I know I seriously tried to stop several times over a four month period before I finally quit. You could say, "Well, Joseph definitely showed poor judgment during those months because he kept picking up." Maybe. But crystal meth profoundly affects the brain. My brain was hijacked during those four months by a terrorist that didn't want to surrender. In those first few weeks, when the brain's cravings are at their peak, we make impulsive decisions without thinking them through—because we literally can't think them through. Our brains are impaired.

Also, users who smoked or injected their crystal, have extremely severe cravings during recovery.

So, yes. If you relapse it's completely natural for you to feel discouraged, even angry. But don't turn that anger on yourself—or others. Turn it toward your disease. Remember, your disease lies to you about your recovery. You have one of the few diseases in the world that tells you, you don't have it.

Which brings us to the next lie your disease wants you to believe...

Lie # 2: My Previous Progress in Recovery Was Wasted

Sometimes, someone who slips will claim in exasperation, "I lost all my clean time. I'm back to day zero. I have to start everything over." That's just how your disease wants you to look at it—as a huge mountain to climb that's so big, you just might as well not even try again. A more accurate way to look it as is: "I have been sober 20 of the past 21 days. Compared to any other three week period before I came into recovery, this is progress."

Yes, you must restart your sobriety clock and establish a new sobriety date, but you don't lose the lessons learned from your previous recovery time. I'd be willing to bet that your previous clean time experience (be it once or a dozen times) probably helped you come back to sobriety faster this time around. We just don't lose all that clean time experience. It stays, working on us from the inside. That's why it's important to remember, even though you reset your sobriety date, your previous clean time counts. It's there, accumulating wisdom.

Sometimes you'll hear an old-timer say something like, "I have X years continuous sobriety." If you ask them why they phrase it that way, they'll respond that when it comes to the "total number" of sober years accumulated, they have much more—and they don't wish to discount that other sobriety time. It's there, just not continuous.

Look at the last several months, or year. If you have more clean time in the last three months than you have relapse time, focus on that. You are definitely heading in the right direction. Don't beat yourself up.

As they say, Rome wasn't built in a day. And a solid program of sobriety usually isn't either.

(Now, having said that, there's this: *there is an emotional, spiritual, and physical growth that only comes with long-term continuous sobriety.* It's something you'll have to experience for yourself.)

Bottom line—none of this is to encourage or excuse relapse, but you need to learn not to demonize relapse, either.

If it never happens to you, great. No one is happier for you than I am. But, if you are involved in any groups of recovering meth addicts, from CMA to rehab to group counseling, you will see people relapse. You may not relapse yourself, but people you care about will. So be kind to yourself and your fellow tweakers who are with you on the journey to sobriety.

Now, get back into the rooms of AA or CMA. Raise your hand when they ask if there are any newcomers. You have nothing to be ashamed of—in fact, you're one of the strongest people in the room at that moment. I'll say it again: recovering addicts are some of the strongest people I know and, when sober, become men and women of amazing character. Our suffering makes us that way.

Lie #3: Since I've Slipped and Already Have to Restart My Sobriety Date, I Might as Well Party One More Time

It starts off simple enough. "I've used and so I've blown it. I've fucked up everything I'd built beforehand in my sobriety and have to start completely over (lie #2); and, since I'm such a general fuck-up of a person with no willpower or moral center (lie #1), I might as well just say 'to hell with it' and party on. I can come back to recovery in a few days, after the run."

There are several problems with this strategy.

▶   How do you know this run is going to be only a few more days? It could last weeks or months or years—until you either die of a heart attack or stroke, or crash your car while nodding off on, say, day 6?

▶   You haven't actually lost all that sobriety gained beforehand; it's still there along with the wisdom gained and lessons learned.

▶   In order to avoid your shame of using in the first place, you see the options as either: a) shaming yourself further by admitting your relapse/failure; or b) continuing to ignore the whole incident and party like it's 1999. In reality, these are not your only options. You could, for example, jettison the self-judgment, realize you had an "acute flare-up" of your chronic disease, and seek immediate treatment like, say, someone with a heart condition would. The big question would then be: given this relapse, what are my treatment options?

Bottom line is: this is one of the most insidious lies because its goal is to keep you using and using, without hope of quitting. The truth is you can stop any time and the sooner you stop the more likely you are to turn this relapse into a powerful lesson (a turn) along your road to recovery (as opposed, to a major car wreck). The disease wants you to keep using until you die. It will try every excuse possible to postpone your quitting, including shame for having used in the first place.

Welcoming Embraces and Cold Shoulders

I'd be remiss if I didn't mention the "cold shoulders" you might receive from some other recovering addicts when they find out you relapsed. You'd think, when it comes to understanding and having compassion, no one would be more accepting than another addict, right? It should be that way and, often, is. There are many welcoming embraces when you come back from "field research," as relapsing is sometimes called in the rooms of CMA.

But the truth is when people react negatively to your relapse, they are merely scared for themselves and coming from a place of fear. Maybe they put you on too high a pedestal. Or maybe someone once advised them to, "Hang around the winners only." And they don't have the broader perception to see that, by coming back to recovery from your slip or relapse, you are indeed an extraordinary winner. It's their loss. Forgive them, then focus on your own recovery.

There are at least two important lessons you get from a cold shoulder. The first is: the opportunity to respond to someone else's fear with compassion. Really, the person turning a cold shoulder needs your kindness and loving compassion now more than you need theirs. They are closing their eyes to the parts of life and recovery they'd rather not see. This is not solid recovery behavior, but old addict behavior. You know, ignore life and pretend it's not there. The second lesson of a cold shoulder is: you'll have more compassion and understanding for others who struggle with relapse in the future. Because you've felt the pain of a cold shoulder, next time it happens to someone you know, you'll reach out a warm embrace and soften your heart to them.

You open your eyes. Open your heart. To yourself and to all others who are struggling with relapses.

7 to 13 times—the average with crystal meth. I hope you are above average. There's no reason you can't be. But if you are not, don't beat yourself up.

And when someone gives you a cold shoulder, remember this: *You are not toxic. What's truly toxic is their thought that makes them respond in fear. Not you, my friend.*

WHAT TO DO

Get Immediately Back into Recovery

The sooner you get back to your recovery the better the odds that you'll make it through this slip to quit successfully. Often, we begin a slip by listening to our disease's favorite lie: "It's only for one night. What can that hurt?" I don't know about you, but I've not met many tweakers who were successful in a one-night stand with crystal meth. (For me, at the end, it was five nights. Every time.)

Another great lie from your disease: "You've already slipped this once, so you might as well do another run. You're going to have to set a new sobriety date anyhow. So what's another few days?"

But is it ever just another few days? Get back to recovery as soon as you can. Don't listen to your disease. Remember, it wants you dead.

Don't Dwell on Shame and Guilt

Infants fall down many times before learning to walk upright, but if they didn't keep trying and falling, they'd crawl forever.

Don't dwell on shame and guilt. Ultimately, excessive guilt is just an ego trip. It's not the end of the world as long as you're back into recovery.

And the most important thing to do is...

Try To Learn From This So It Won't Happen Again

Hello? When did this relapse really begin? Here's a hint: the relapse began long before you picked up the pipe, straw, or syringe.

It may have begun when you started flirting with old triggers—certain people, places, or things. Or maybe you started missing meetings. Then you began listening to the lies your disease whispered. You romanticized using and the cravings quickly overwhelmed you. All of this occurred before you picked up the drug itself.

Carefully examine how this relapse came to be, so you don't unknowingly repeat it.

APPENDIX

Resources

Quitting Crystal Meth – The Blog

My website and blog where the conversation about "living the full and free life beyond meth and addiction" continues. I invite you to visit often and let me hear from you:

> quittingcrystalmeth.com

Crystal Meth Anonymous

The first place to go when trying to find a local meeting or connect with other recovering addicts is CMA's website:

> crystalmethanonymous.com

Other Organizations/Websites

Narcotics Anonymous info can be found at:

> na.org

Then, there's the mothership, Alcoholics Anonymous:

> aa.org

And for gay men specifically:
>tweaker.org

Further Reading

Clean: Overcoming Addiction and Ending America's Greatest Tradgedy by David Sheff (Eamon Dolan/Houghton Mifflin Harcourt, 2013). Based on the latest research in psychology, neuroscience, and medicine, *Clean* offers clear counsel for parents and others who want to prevent drug problems and for addicts and their loved ones no matter what stage of the illness they're in.

Crystal Clear: Stories of Hope (published by Crystal Meth Anonymous, 2011). CMA's first publication, this is a collection of personal stories and essays on doing the 12 Steps CMA style. 109 easily readable pages.

Overcoming Crystal Meth Addiction by Steven J. Lee, M.D. (Marlowe & Company, 06). This exhaustive book covers a lot of excellent information, including harm reduction and the psychology of addiction. Because of it's length, over 300 pages, I think it's more for the professional in the recovery field or the very motivated addict/reader who wants a broader view of crystal meth beyond the "how to" of quitting.

The Velvet Rage by Alan Downs, Ph.D. (Da Capo Lifelong Books, 2nd ed. 2012). If you are a gay man, this book might be considered a must read. Offering practical and inspired strategies to stop the cycle of avoidance and self-defeating behavior, *The Velvet Rage* passionately explores the stages of a gay man's journey out of shame.

About Joseph Sharp

Joseph is author of *Quitting Crystal Meth: What to Expect & What to Do* (CreateSpace, 2013), *Living Our Dying* (Hyperion '96, translated into Chinese, Japanese, Spanish, German) and *Spiritual Maturity* (Penguin 2002, translated into Spanish). He has worked as a dishwasher, short order cook, legal secretary and chaplain for the Infectious Disease Unit at Parkland Memorial Hospital in Dallas, Texas. Living with HIV since 1982, a survivor of cancer, and recovering crystal meth addict, Joseph hangs his hat in Palm Springs, California.

To contact Joseph visit quittingcrystalmeth.com.

On Facebook at Facebook.com/QuittingCrystalMeth.

Twitter @QuittingMeth.

To buy more books visit amazon.com or your local recovery bookstore.

49523819R00070

Made in the USA
Charleston, SC
27 November 2015